COMMUNITY FOR LIFE

COMMUNITY FOR LIFE

ULRICH EGGERS

Foreword by

John A. Hostetler

WITHDRAWN

HERALD PRESS
Scottdale, Pennsylvania
Kitchener, Ontario
1988

Library of Congress Cataloging-in-Publication Data

Eggers, Ulrich, 1955-
    Community for life.

    Translation of: Gemeinschaft—lebenslänglich.
    Bibliography: p.
    1. Hutterian Brethren (Rifton, N.Y.)   2. Eggers,
Ulrich, 1955-   .   3. Rifton (N.Y.)—Description.
4. Rifton (N.Y.)—Church history.   I.   Title.
BX8129.B634R54313   1988   289.7'74734   87-17817
ISBN 0-8361-3451-6 (pbk.)

Photo credits: pages 65, 66 (bottom), 68 (top), 70 (bottom), 71 (bottom
right), 72 (top), 138, 139, 140 (bottom), 141 (bottom), 142 (bottom), and 143
(top) by Plough Publishing House; pages 68 (bottom), 69 (top and bottom
right), 70 (top), 137 (bottom), and 141 (top) by Christel Eggers; cover and
pages 66 (top), 67, 69 (bottom left), 71 (top and bottom left), 72 (bottom),
137 (top), 140 (top), 142 (top), 143 (bottom), and 144 by Ulrich Eggers.

94 93 92 91 90 89 88 10 9 8 7 6 5 4 3 2 1

Contents

Foreword

Community for Life is an engaging, colorful, and personalized account of the bruderhof movement, surpassing in information, tone, and spiritual perception all the previous analytical studies by either insiders or outsiders.

If community life in all its spiritual connotations can be put into words, this account has come the closest. The reader feels included in a wide scope of activity and perceptions—the odors, heat, scenery, frustrations, the feelings between children and parents, and the reasons for lifelong commitment.

This book is the first to treat the historical backgrounds, the ups and downs of community life, and the difficulties of the past with the support of bruderhof informants.

The bruderhof movement originated in 1920 during a period of social unrest and spiritual searching in Germany. The mere articulation of disillusionment and the rejection of middle-class values was not sufficient for Eberhard Arnold (1883-1935), a deeply converted Christian man. Eberhard and his wife, Emmy, determined to follow the teaching and commandments of Jesus.

With a few adults and their children the Arnolds began living in community, holding no private property and living in complete faith in Jesus. Others joined them, including students, teachers, workers, and poor people from German, English, Swiss, American, and Swedish backgrounds. From Sannerz in the Rhön district south of Fulda, they moved to a larger farm called the Rhön bruderhof in 1927.

On learning that there were Hutterites in North America who descended from sixteenth-century Anabaptism, Arnold visited their communities in the United States and Canada during 1930-1931. In all major beliefs and practices, the two groups agreed. The community founded by Arnold in Germany was accepted into the Hutterian Church, and Eberhard Arnold was ordained as a Servant of the Word by the Hutterite elders.

In 1933, the new community in Germany came under the scrutiny of the Nazi government. Their school was provided with a Nazi teacher and their men faced conscription into the military service. To provide shelter for the children a second location was founded in Liechtenstein in 1934. In the following year on November 22, 1935, Eberhard Arnold died.

The bruderhof in Germany was dissolved by the Gestapo. Three members were imprisoned and others were allowed to leave the country. Some moved to Liechtenstein, while the rest went to Holland and eventually England, where a bruderhof in Cotswold had been started in 1936. All remaining members came together in England by 1938. The community grew rapidly, numbering about 350 people in 1940.

But Britain during this time wished to free itself of all German elements. To avoid the internment of themselves as enemy aliens, the bruderhof moved to Paraguay, the only country offering them religious freedom. But a small group remained at the Cotswold bruderhof, and in fact continued to increase as more English people joined the community there.

For twenty years the Paraguayan bruderhof communities lived on a property named Primavera. Here they experienced poverty and isolation, and lacking the original decisive leadership of Eberhard Arnold, "fell away." Conditions in Paraguay brought their relationships with the Hutterite colonies to the breaking point in 1955.

The Paraguayan communities moved to the United States in 1954, 1961, and 1962. Their five current communities are Woodcrest at Rifton, New York; New Meadow Run at Farmington, Pennsylvania; Deer Spring at Norfolk, Connecticut; Darvell at Robertsbridge, Sussex, England; and Pleasant View at Ulster Park, New York.

Following the restoration of formal relationships with the Hutterian Brethren groups in 1974, the bruderhof movement changed its name to the Hutterian Society of Brothers. Since 1986 they have adopted in full the name "Hutterian Brethren." The five communities support themselves by the manufacture of children's equipment known as Community Playthings and Rifton Equipment for the Handicapped.

The author asks himself, "How in the world can anyone live like this?" The bruderhof members reply again and again, "Surrender yourself completely. Your wishes, your plans, your ideas all have to die every day." Self-surrender, the community insists, is not a call to severe asceticism, personal suppression, or a restricted lifestyle as perceived by those who try in their own strength. To die to self is to find yourself. For the bruderhof people, the author says, it works. Yet it remains a deep mystery. "Paradoxically, the personality grows, becomes richer, more rounded, more perfect, if the ego dies."

The details of community living touch a wide range of activity: the attitude toward children, the special celebrations, the nightwatchman and his songs, the many guests, the meaning of silence, the law of love, the beards, grooming, and blend of old Hutterite dress with modified practices among both men and women.

Each day one has to learn anew how to live in community. The bruderhof community, says the author, does not consist of nice people, exciting midday meals, and colorful folklore. Rather, it represents a mastery of normal daily life. Work is quiet and concentrated, not hectic. One works for others, not for a boss.

During most of its 67-year history, the bruderhof movement has been reluctant to assist writers who wished to describe their community life—more reluctant than traditional Hutterites or Amish communities. This reluctance has often been cause for offense. Scholars wanted to know: Did the group have things to hide? Did they wish to control their own public image?

The answers, as this book points out, lie elsewhere. The crises and struggles within the community are not talked about indiscriminately. The mistakes and scars of the past cannot be forgiven and forgotten if they are constantly stirred up and uncovered. The high sensitivity of Ulrich Eggers, combined with the support of informants in the bruderhof communities, signals a new milestone.

—John A. Hostetler, Director
Center for Anabaptist and Pietist Studies
Elizabethtown College (Pennsylvania)

Community for Life

*Unless a kernel of wheat falls to the ground
and dies, it remains only a single seed.
But if it dies, it produces many seeds.
—John 12:21, NIV.*

1

Weary Travelers

There we were—my wife, Christel, our friend Kalle, and I—3,700 miles from home. We stood in the dusty afternoon heat at the bus station of New Paltz, New York, next to a small heap of luggage and a few other passengers. An Adirondack Trailways bus had brought us to this tired little town founded many years ago by French Huguenot settlers.

We were searching for a small but living bit of German church history, a bruderhof of the Hutterian Brethren. This Christian community was established in 1920 in the Rhön Mountains of Germany by a young theologian named Eberhard Arnold. After a tortuous series of events it found itself in the United States. At this particular bruderhof four hundred people, young and old, were actually living the message of the Sermon on the Mount and not only talking about it. At least that's what we had been told.

Three hours ago we had left the gigantic bus terminal of New York City and the feverish hustle of 42nd Street. We had wormed our way through a tunnel beneath Manhattan and the Hudson River. Finally we had left the endless and ugly suburbs behind us, dominated by advertising billboards and high-tension wires crazily crisscrossing the highway, and the endless shopping centers cropping up from nowhere. We had managed to escape the gray haze of an immense concrete landscape.

Before us lay gently sloping hills and lovely green woods—a pastoral view we had hardly hoped to see after the enormous, fascinating, yet nerve-racking city. But even here from time to time gigantic billboards intruded among the trees announcing, "McDonalds welcomes buses at Exit 19," or whatever.

New York had nearly finished us off. It had been a strenuous flight from our native Germany, with six hours difference in time. As we jolted over the rough highways, we longed for nothing more than a bit of peace, a room with a closed door, and a cold drink with tinkling ice cubes. America!

But this was not to be—at least not yet. When we finally managed to squeeze out of the bus with its unpleasant odor of incense, the heat nearly knocked us over. The blacktop of the parking lot was sizzling in the sun. Why had no one told us that we might encounter this kind of humid tropical heat in June? Coming from the mild climate of northern Germany, how could I survive any length of time out here? Not even the rather sparse-looking structure of the bus station with its big clock and the stars and stripes above its gable seemed to offer any protection. Who in the world had come up with the absurd idea of traveling to this place, anyway? How would I survive the strenuous welcome ceremony ahead, especially struggling with my poor English?

We sit down trying to keep cool. We are impatient with the heat. Beads of perspiration slide down our backs. We decide to phone. But where is the telephone? Ah, there! On the right side of the building a phone booth is attached to the wall. So I find the number for "Hutterian Brethren, Woodcrest Bruderhof, Rifton." When I try to lift the receiver, I find that only loose wires are dangling down the left side of the booth. Well, I'll look for another phone!

Inside the building at a few wobbling tables a number of young people are sipping their colas. Sure enough, there on the wall is another telephone. I lift the receiver and listen. Nothing happens. I read the instructions. Now—lift the receiver. Ah yes! Insert 25 cents. It works. The dial tone hums. The number—wait, area code? Dial zero or one? Looks like zero. I try 0-914-558—bother, wrong again! 0-914-658-3141. Yes, that works. But nothing happens. I listen patiently. Nothing! I put the receiver down. I try once more. Again nothing happens.

Slowly the young people at the table begin to notice me. How awful! I can't even handle a telephone call in the United States. What's the matter? I'm not from the back-woods, am I? I read the instructions for the third time. So that's it. I should have dialed l first. Okay, here we go: l-914—there! I can hear a beep, then a voice: "Would youpleasedepositseventyfivecentsforthenextthreeminutes." Oh, I beg your pardon! I didn't understand a word. The shock makes me put down the receiver again. The young people throw interested glances. Nothing like this has happened to me before. I hope they don't come over to help me. I wouldn't understand them at all!

It's best that I go to the restroom now. I need a break from the phone to gather courage. Christel and Kalle sit outside on the veranda and wait. Great, at least I've found cool water in the restroom. Now then, back to the telephone! Man alive, I ought to find a way. So here we go: 1-914— Sure enough, this time I can understand at least half of what is said. Another 75 cents goes down the slot and now it actually rings somewhere. Then a voice—fresh, young, and clear—answers "Hutterian Brethren . . . oh, yes, welcome! We've been waiting for you. Where are you? Yes, we'll pick you up! Right away!" Relieved and truly thankful I put the receiver down and immediately feel not quite so deserted in this gigantic country.

Noticeably reassured, I walk outside. "It worked. They are picking us up!" As I sit down with the others on the bench, slouching against the backrest quite relieved, I realize that my shirt and jeans are dripping wet. Excitement and heat. Carefully I stretch out on the bench. Now we must wait. My thoughts begin to wander. A strange feeling, slightly unreal: *Here we sit on a bench, waiting far away from home, seemingly very normal, and yet. . . .*

How did it actually all begin? Was it that book about— no, the telephone call—or yes, it was at the music festival in England. At the festival I was looking through some newly published books stacked on a big table there. I knew more or less what titles I wanted. Then I saw the small table with pamphlets and paperbacks about Mennonites. There were other books too. One title read, *Torches Together: The Life and Story of the Bruderhof Communities.* Bruderhof? That sounded German. Why was it on this table of English publications? Let's see. Photos: "The Rhön Bruderhof," people dressed in the style of the German youth movement of the 1920s sitting on a hilltop, viewing the countryside. I was captivated almost immediately. Yes, that's how it began. Instead of a heap of new publications, I returned with a single book: *Torches Together,* by Emmy Arnold, purchased at a small book-stand from an elderly lady who wore a polka-dotted black-and-white kerchief.

Emmy Arnold and Eberhard Arnold—I encountered their names for the first time. These two people had been active at a wild and stormy time in Germany's history. The First World War was lost. Revolution raged on the street. Disappointment, political listlessness, and hunger were rampant—but also a search for new ways. Radical movements arose. The German youth movement was at its height. In the midst of it all, young theologian Eberhard Arnold turned to an unconditional pacifism because of his experience with war. He dreamed and planned and began a new nonviolent commune dedicated to taking the Sermon on the Mount of the New Testament literally.

Again and again I am stunned by the similarities of Germany then to our present-day situation. Hopelessness, fear, depression compete with new ideas, new ways, and the breaking of new ground. *Torches Together,* the story of the Hutterian Brethren, the story of Eberhard Arnold. It is not only history. It is highly contemporary. He reflects our situation, our questions, our problems—and perhaps even offers us answers.

Back in Germany I looked for more books on Eberhard Arnold. How disappointing! There was hardly anything. He seemed to be forgotten. I looked in the encyclopedia. Yes, there was something on him. Born July 26, 1883, son of theologian Carl Franklin Arnold in Breslau. A well-situated middle-class background. In 1909 Eberhard Arnold earned his Ph.D. in Philosophy. But these were only dry facts. Now where did the exciting story of his efforts to establish an early Christian community begin?

Bit by bit I continued plowing through the book. It was slow going for me since it was written in English. I had not yet read half of it, when I discovered another bruderhof-related book. I was looking through a tattered box of old books, odds and ends, at a secondhand bookstore in Hamburg. There were stacks of books at ridiculously low prices. The books looked like it too—garbage! But then a thin volume caught my eye. *Joan Mary Fry, the Sacrament of Life*, Neuwerk Publishing House, Schlüchtern. I had just read about that! It was the publishing house which Arnold directed at his first bruderhof in Sannerz, Germany.

A week later I found myself at a flea market in a shopping center. A housewife behind a table had a basketful of secondhand books for sale. Since I am an inveterate bookworm, I could not pass by without digging into it. Seconds later I picked out a light-blue volume, *The History of the DCSV*. I had just read about that too—the German Student Christian Movement. Arnold had served as its longtime secretary! Quickly I checked the index at the back. Sure enough, Eberhard Arnold's name appeared several times in the text. After the book changed owners for a ludicrously low price, I began to feel rather strange. This could not be coincidence.

In the meantime I had read enough in Emmy Arnold's book to decide to ask the bruderhof's publishing house in America for permission to translate portions of her book in our periodical. People simply had to read this.

A week later, three of us—my wife, our friend Britta, and I—were in our small kitchen preparing lunch together. Just as I was telling them enthusiastically about *Torches*

Together and reading some interesting passages to them, the telephone rang. I lifted the receiver. A deep voice with a slight American accent answered in German, "Hello, this is Hermann Arnold from the bruderhof. We are on a visit in Germany. Our publishing house in America has just phoned your letter through to me. Therefore, I thought I'd call on you. . . ."

I felt weak in the knees. It seemed as if history was catching up with me. From the telephone conversation I learned that Hermann Arnold, a nephew of Eberhard, joined the bruderhof in 1935. He explained briefly about the Hutterian Society of Brothers. He mentioned Michael Holzack's book about the Canadian Hutterites, *Das Vergessene Volk*. This was a surprise bestseller in the secular market of mainly atheist Germany. Portions of it had just appeared in our periodical. I remembered that in the back of *Torches Together* I had just read that in 1974 the Society of Brothers reunited with the Hutterites.

I wondered what kind of person was sitting at the other end of the telephone line. "Yes, Michael Holzach is right in many things." "And sad to say, much of what he wrote is true. We dress as they dress," Hermann Arnold explained. "This expresses our unity. But in some ways we are different from the Canadian brothers. We have joined the Hutterites because we do not want to be one of the many small religious sects."

It was hard for me to believe that I was having this conversation. Four weeks ago I knew nothing about the Society of Brothers and Eberhard Arnold. Now I was speaking with one of his relatives. He told me about the group's years in Paraguay, the only country that would accept them in 1940 after they had to flee Germany. "We were hungry then," he said. "That was our time in the desert, inwardly and outwardly a hard time."

Then he told me that he had just delivered a translated manuscript of *Torches Together* to a publishing house. In a few months the book would appear here in Germany. Someone had secured German-language rights to it before me . . . . . "By the way, Eberhard Arnold's sister lives here in Hamburg, a deaconess by the name of Hannah Arnold," he continued. "She belongs to a church— Wait a minute. What was the name? Holstenwall, I think. Do you happen to know her?"

I was no longer surprised at anything. "Yes," I answered. "I know the church. It is the one we go to. I have heard the name Hannah Arnold, but I didn't know . . . ."

"Guess who just phoned me?" I said when I returned to the kitchen.

A few days later I received a fat package of books about the bruderhof. All were printed by Plough Publishing House operated by the four Arnoldian bruderhofs in existence today—three in the United States and one in England.

Slowly my thoughts return to the present. Kalle and Cristel are taking a good look at every car that stops at the bus station. What are the bruderhofers going to be like? Is that them? I keep remembering Michael Holzach's book. I think of the severe moral demands of the Canadian Hutterites, their isolated communities, their religious services that last hours on end, and their monotonous songs with more than a hundred verses. And I remember that no flowers are permitted on the Western Hutterian bruderhof because they are considered a "lust of the eye." So are pictures on the wall and colorful clothing. They are so strict it must be depressing.

Of course, I remind myself, they are not like that here. But how are they then? I remember something a friend told me who had visited the Woodcrest bruderhof a few years ago. "Ah, well, it is quite interesting," he said, "but the people are not quite up-to-date. Everything reminds you a bit of how it was in the twenties in Germany, as if time had stood still."

I try to imagine what the people of the New York bruderhof are like—a mixture of strict Hutterites, normal churchgoers, and people of the folk-dancing German youth movement.

Oh, no, that can't be them in that clanky tin box of a car up there? I can't imagine they would have such a car? That can't be one of their young women crossing the parking lot diagonally and heading for us with a cigarette in her hand. The people of the bruderhof don't smoke. They clashed with the Old Hutterites over that in 1937. For a time in the early days they were united with the Hutterian Church. But smoking and loud laughing were some of the reasons for a separation.

Another car approaches. No, that can't be them either. Surely they'll come with a minibus. That is more Hutterian. Or perhaps with an open truck with several sacks of wheat in the back. Time passes. My thoughts wander.

Additional "coincidences" were responsible for the fact that we were now sitting here. As a follow-up to the reprint we had made of Michael Holzach's book on the Hutterites, we had published an interview with the young author. We did this two months before his tragic death in a flooded river near Dortmund. We had visited Holzach in an old farmhouse on the Lüneburger Heide. He lived there with his friend, a dog named Feldmann, mentioned extensively in his other bestselling book, "*Deutschland-umsonst*" (about his tour through Germany on foot without money). He had moved into this old villa among the heather as caretaker, rent-free, except that occasionally he showed the house to prospective buyers. Here he was shielded for the most part from the press which had shown more and more interest in him.

We talked a long time about his stay with the Hutterites. One could sense how deeply this experience had moved him. He showed his Hutterian cap—with a feather added, which of course was prohibited and frowned upon as a "lust of the eyes." He told us how much he liked the hand-sewn shirts and trousers from his time with the Hutterites, and how much he enjoyed wearing them and that these things gave him a feeling of home and security.

Later we told him of our discovery of the new Arnoldian Hutterites with roots in the German Christian youth movement. "I know them," he answered, taking a book from his shelf: *Salt and Light*, by Eberhard Arnold. He told us that he knew the whole story. On Holzach's walk through Germany, he had even tried to find the old Rhön bruderhof, but without success. So once again we had encountered Eberhard Arnold unexpectedly.

Later we met someone who had actually been at the original Society of Brothers. We heard firsthand impressions. I received more information on the bruderhofs when I discovered the address of an old man who had gone to the Rhön bruderhof, in 1932 as a young unemployed worker. It was a hard time for young city folk who came to work at the Rhön bruderhof where people lived simply and ascetically.

All this was quite interesting to me professionally because I am the editor of a youth magazine concerned with radical, up-to-date Christianity. But it appealed to me personally also. To take the Sermon on the Mount seriously, to live more radically, not to value everything according to its price, to live simply, a lifestyle of responsibility toward the world, nonviolence—all these were concerns about which I had reflected a great deal and which I would like to put into practice. That is why I had always been interested in contemporary models.

Now I was fascinated with the lively mixture of radicalism, of nostalgic attraction to the youth movement of the twenties, and an adventurous history of a people who had lived a radical primitive Christianity for several generations in community of goods. Moreover, I had always wanted to visit the United States. Until now this venture was hindered by the high cost of travel and the wish to live simply. But this was my chance. Not simply tourism but everything close to my heart, the issues of our time, my questions. . . . I sent a letter to Woodcrest.

A few weeks later the answer came. The brother responsible for visits and guests asked for more details. In my nostalgic dreams about the bruderhof, I had hoped to work somewhere on the farm. At long last something other than a desk! But now I learned that the Eastern bruderhofs do practically no farming at all and that we would be put to work at something else. We received a printed guest letter with brief information on the life of the bruderhof and many warnings—sugar cube and whip.

"The bruderhof has an open door for all. But no one should remain a guest," they wrote. "We only recognize co-workers. Through working together one gets to know the other much better and learns something about the nature of our life together. We expect that all who come to us are seeking and questioning people. Anyone who does not seek with us and does not ask about our community, we shall ask what he is looking for and why he is here. All guests are warned against making a hasty and premature judgment about us. We do not want to have anyone among us who comes only out of intellectual interest. Anyone who is opposed to the witness and truth of the prophets and apostles, the early Christians, and the Hutterites, cannot stay with us." A little rebuffed, we still decided to go.

Now it is time for someone from the bruderhof to pick us up! And finally they do. A blue Dodge minibus (with air-conditioning, wow!) drives in. Yes, here they are. Two men step from the car. The one in a green shirt, suspenders, somewhat heavy shoes, and a beard—looking like a senior forest ranger—is Hermann Arnold. He is the man I had visited with by phone in Germany. He had traveled all the way from the New Meadow Run bruderhof in Pennsylvania specifically to meet us here at the New York bruderhof. He was our loyal companion for the next few weeks.

With him, in a bright blue shirt, darkly tanned and the incarnation of a true German, was Danni Meier—actually a likable Swiss in his mid-forties. Oh yes, he must be a son of Hans Meier, who after the dissolution of the Rhön bruderhof by the SS, was imprisoned for three months. Only by the skin of his teeth had Hans managed to escape a concentration camp. Again history was catching up with the present.

2

A Leap of Faith

Until Eberhard Arnold's sixteenth year there was no hint that he might ever found an alternative commune. True, he had always felt drawn to the poor and underprivileged fringe of humanity, much to the chagrin of his affluent parents. He found these people to be more genuine, more warmhearted than the conventional upper-middle class to which his parents belonged. But such revolutionary thoughts as would later come to expression did not even occur to him at this age.

It all began in Berlin with Eberhard's uncle, a Protestant minister. This man lived a convincing, practical Christianity and actively supported the poor in his parish, Eberhard encountered for the first time a Christian who was completely different from his parents with their middle-class religiosity.

Eberhard wanted to know. What was the wellspring of his uncle's refreshing and committed life? With vigor Eberhard began the search. He talked with others, considered, doubted, read the Bible, and finally found the way to Christ—an encounter which turned Eberhard's whole life upside down.

His newfound faith had immediate consequences. He went to all his teachers and apologized for his dishonesty in copying from his classmates. But he found little understanding. One of his high school teachers made fun of Eberhard and dismissed the repentant youth from his class. This didn't seem to bother Eberhard much. Only a short time later, while still a sixteen-year-old, his name appeared as a speaker on public notices distributed by the Salvation Army, to whom he felt drawn. Their Christianity and social action rang true.

One can imagine the indignation of Eberhard's parents when they saw the bold type, "Attention! Salvation Army! Tonight missionary Eberhard Arnold will speak—everybody is warmly invited!" They felt ashamed of their troublesome son. His father feared that his own position as a university professor might be endangered through the activities of his son. He was embarrassed by Eberhard's missionary efforts at school. Finally his parents sent him to the small Silesian city of Jauer to finish high school there in peace and quiet.

How serious Eberhard was in his enthusiasm is apparent in a memoir of his youth. He wrote it in third person.

> Bad days ensued, when the parents held their biannual big parties. Because of these Eberhard attacked his parents: "Father, I hear that the food and drink for this party will cost more than 200 marks. Those invited are nearly all wealthier than we are. They all have plenty to eat at home. They in turn will invite you and offer you expensive wines and roasts and desserts. But I know of poor and innocent families in the east of the city who do not have enough money to supply their children with milk. You all know

that Jesus said, 'If you plan a banquet, do not invite your friends and relatives who will invite you in turn, but go to the highways and invite the poorest of the poor, who will never be able to invite you.' You go to church and worship, but is this life of injustice from God or is it from the devil?"

The wrath of the father over the impudent son was indescribable. How could Eberhard show such disrespect to his own father, who was showered with honors by the highest church officials? He locked Eberhard in his room for several days.

To take the Bible literally, to draw consequences, to act, even if it would bring disadvantages and would be costly— that would characterize Arnold's future life.

After he finally graduated, Eberhard began to study theology. Young people gathered around him as he continued to speak at conferences of the revival movement. Whole cities turned upside down with the message of spiritual renewal within traditional, insipid Christianity. In one of these meetings, in 1907, Eberhard Arnold was introduced to Emmy von Hollander. Both sensed quickly that they had much in common. Three weeks later they were engaged, drawn together in the search for active and committed Christianity. Emmy Arnold wrote:

> Both our parents in particular were unable to understand our revolutionary attitude regarding social questions and the question of the church. For it became very clear to us that the so-called world church stood on a completely false foundation because it accepted children into the church just on the basis of their birthright when in fact only those should receive baptism who have taken the step of faith.

Eberhard and Emmy decided to face the consequences

and ask to be baptized again as adults. Their parents were strongly opposed. At all costs, they wanted to stop their children from taking this unusual step of faith. The situation became even more tense when Eberhard was barred from taking his final examination in theology. This was because he stated clearly that he would never enter the service of the state church.

Eberhard's faith was becoming costly. Emmy's parents warned their daughter that her intended husband was "irresponsible" and obviously unable to supply a decent financial foundation for a family. Eberhard changed to a philosophy major. In November 1909 he received his Ph.D. in Philosophy. The same morning Eberhard and Emmy visited Emmy's father and requested the necessary documents for a civil wedding ceremony. On December 20, 1909, they married. By the beginning of the First World War, three children had arrived—Emy-Margret, Hardy, and Heini. Their lives also would be closely linked to the history of the bruderhofs.

At the outbreak of the First World War, Eberhard was called to his reserve unit. Germany was caught up in a wave of patriotic enthusiasm against their archenemies, France and England." May God punish them," Germany's sons went singing to their death. Eberhard, not fully recovered from severe TB of the lungs, was released after two weeks of service. But those days gave him enough time to think deeply.

Christians on both sides were shooting at each other. This in spite of their belief that community among Christians is more powerful than nationality and can reach across national borders.

Was entering the ambulance service the only alternative

for Christians? Eberhard Arnold wasn't sure, but the first deep doubt was sown.

In 1915 he took over the literary direction of the Furche Publishing House. Part of his responsibility was to edit the small periodical of the German Student Christian Movement, *Die Fürche* (The Furrow). During wartime, publications of the Furche Publishing House were strongly colored with German nationalism in support of the war. Christians were asked to rally to the "just cause"—but the just cause turned into a desperate struggle of survival. The war took a terrible toll of human and material resources. The newspaper columns listing the names of the war heroes killed at the front grew longer. At home people began to go hungry. Food was severely rationed.

The more difficult the situation became, the more depressing was the mood in the country. Embittered people realized that even in this desperate time of war the rich and those of privileged position had enough of everything, while common people went hungry. In the army it was the same. The officers behind the front lived in plenty while the foot soldiers had to be satisfied with very little.

Because of his work in the German Student Christian Movement, Eberhard had access to the military hospitals. Through many conversations with disillusioned soldiers, his doubts increased. Is war a legitimate political tool? How is it possible for Christians, or any person for that matter, to say yes to this evil?

With the final collapse of the war effort in 1918, Germany fell into a deep national depression. Repressed anger and disappointment resulted in widespread disillusionment. The Kaiser fled into exile in Holland. Everyone looked toward the future with fear. The self-reliance of the whole nation was demolished. How could life go on?

Disappointment and anger exploded into revolution in November 1918. Berlin experienced civil war. A workers' council and a soldiers' council were installed. A new government was being formed. Eberhard and Emmy were present in the big hall of the "Busch" in Berlin when the Social Democrat Ebert was proclaimed the new president of the Reich. Excited discussions took place.

Voices cried out: "Where was God in 1914? Where were the Christians? Why did you join in? Why did the clergy bless the weapons?" Eberhard and Emmy were deeply impressed by these questions. Was it not necessary for Christians to have a completely different attitude?

The collapse of Germany was especially hard for the youth. Their future now seemed totally blocked. How would things develop? Did everything have to change? What values could they still hold? What was the meaning of their existence?

A great search for new ways began. Groups formed. People met in homes to talk things over. Conferences were held. A whole generation was on the move—but where to?

Eberhard and Emmy took part in these discussions. Again and again Eberhard spoke at large gatherings of German youth. All branches of the youth movement were represented in these open evening meetings. Christians, atheists, members of the Student Christian Movement, and Baptists became so caught up in their discussions that they began to meet twice a week. Until late into the night they read Tolstoy and Dostoevski. They wrestled with profound issues, but the answers were not easy to come by.

The youth movement which began at the turn of the

century with the Wandervögel, and the Free German youth, flourished now. With a new generation, a new way was being found. They met together in conferences and on hikes, sat around campfires, sang and made music. They dressed simply, peasant-like, and found new joy in nature. Idealistic and romantic plans were hashed out, the beginnings of a classless new culture. People wanted to free themselves from the conventional ties of middle-class life. The materialism of the past would be banned forever.

But the great alternative, the completely new way, was not achieved. Tempted by the values preached by national socialism, only a decade later a great part of the youth movement fell for the new myth of the people and the fatherland and were assimilated into Hitler's youth organization.

Eberhard Arnold and his close associates lived in the style of the youth movement and were revolutionary in outlook. But from the beginning they were determined to find a true purpose, something to hold on to. In this search Eberhard quickly encountered the Sermon on the Mount.

In 1919, at a conference of the German Christian Student Movement on the Frauenberg near Marburg, he gave a hotly debated lecture about Jesus' Sermon on the Mount. One of the participants remembers:

> The focus of all that was said and thought was Jesus' Sermon on the Mount. Eberhard Arnold burned it into our hearts with a passionate spirituality, hammered it into our wills with prophetic power and the tremendous mobile force of his whole personality. This was the Sermon on the Mount in the full force of its impact, in its absolute and undiminished relevance, its unconditional absoluteness. Here there was no compromise. Whoever wants to belong to this

kingdom must give himself wholly and go through with it to the last!

In August of the same year Arnold spoke on the theme "Can a Christian be a soldier?" His answer, a clear "No," led to a heated discussion. A report from this student conference quoted Arnold as saying:

> The Christian should be a continuous corrective and conscience for the state, a leaven, a foreign body. We cannot be soldiers, executioners, or police officers. It is our task to witness in word and deed that nothing of Jesus' words be twisted. We have to obey God more than men! We have to be a corrective in this world.

Arnold's words hit like a bolt of lightning and of course met with strong opposition.

Arnold's work was also controversial with the Furche Publishing House and with the German Student Christian Movement. There were two camps—those who wanted to reform the old and fill it with a new content, and others, like Eberhard Arnold, who believed that something completely new, something revolutionary, inspired by the spirit of the Sermon on the Mount was necessary. Arnold's views were reflected increasingly in the publications of the Furche Publishing House and in the groups to which he related.

The circle around Eberhard Arnold grew larger. The question became more and more urgent: "How can the new understanding of the Sermon on the Mount—how can the new way—find practical expression?" They considered establishing settlements for adults. Eberhard and Emmy thought of traveling through Germany by wagon, helping the sick, singing together, playing music, and teaching their children on the way. They would remain in one place as long as help was needed and then move on. A decisive idea came to them at an open evening meeting while studying the happenings of Pentecost in the Bible—Community of Faith, Community of Love, Community of Goods. This was the answer to their deep-felt needs!

The witness of the early Christians in the book of Acts would be their example. The direction they would follow was to live together, to work together, and to have everything in common.

Soon they started looking for feasible locations for this new form of living together. Because housing was limited in the cities, they were not considered as possibilities. Eberhard traveled extensively to find a suitable place somewhere in the country. At this time the group around Eberhard Arnold was not the only one exploring the possibilities of patterning their lives after the early church.

During the Whitsun conference in Schlüchtern in 1920, Arnold's group found an opportunity to visit the already existing settlement at the Habertshof. The simple life and modest style of dress, influenced by the youth movement, and the undemanding attitude of the people there in their life together left a deep impression on Eberhard and Emmy. It was similar to how they imagined their own life in community.

At the end of this conference the Arnolds, with a few others, took a walk to the nearby village of Sannerz, where a rather large building stood empty. This brick structure of fifteen rooms seemed to be well suited for their purpose. The stables and surrounding fields and orchards were also available. The owner of the house was ready to sell but hadn't made up his mind about the price. So they returned to Berlin without making a deal.

The situation in the Furche Publishing House became more and more difficult. Eberhard and Emmy were increasingly frustrated with the fruitless discussions which led nowhere. The situation cried out for action. "Let's not waste words any longer," they said. "Something must be done!"

As would happen many times in the following years, the Arnolds and their friends took a leap of faith. They sent a telegram on June 21, 1920, and set out for their new home. It was a journey into an unknown future, since negotiations for buying the house were not completed.

That's how the Sannerz bruderhof began. During the first year of its existence more than 3,000 guests were welcomed to its three small rooms in the back of an inn belonging to Lotzenius. A long journey had begun with this bold first step.

3

Kerchieves, Beards, and Suspenders

Hermann and Danni speak German. I feel a little more relaxed and sheltered. We are sitting on the roomy back seat of the Dodge van, limply stretching our arms and legs. My shirt, wet from perspiration, begins slowly to dry out. We have just left the last houses of New Paltz behind us and are traveling north on the main road to Rifton. Meadows alternate with small areas of woods. Occasionally a naked rock crops up from the hills around, and then again there is woodland.

There's a lot of countryside. It's rather lonely for a "city on a hill which cannot be hid," I think to myself. But the first bruderhof in Sannerz, Germany, also was not a public attraction and yet it had many guests.

It must have been quite lively and moving there in Sannerz. I remember a few anecdotes which I read in Emmy Arnold's book. Shortly after the small community was able to rent the large brick building in Sannerz and had purchased some furniture, the first visitors arrived.

"Young people from every background, come and

unite!" seemed to be the watchword then. At the same time, to find food and lodging for all of them was not easy. Many were able to stay in the barn of the neighboring farmer. Food consisted of porridge and vegetable soup, which was watered down according to the number of guests. Many were strict vegetarians which caused a problem when they would only eat raw vegetables or fresh fruit.

The small community especially enjoyed the periodic visits of a traveling musician, Hans Fiehler. He always wore a red cap, shorts, and a red waistcoat on which was embroidered in big letters "Hans im Glück" (Hans in Luck). Four ocarinas (a type of flute made of clay), named Great Grandmother, Grandmother, Mother, and Child, as well as two violins, accompanied him on his journey. Wherever he played, he drew a large audience. For "Hans in Luck" the bruderhof must have been like a second home.

Sometimes opera singers, habitual drinkers, or tramps would also visit. One day a whole family arrived at the door, each child dressed like a different flower from the forest. This was the time of the youth movement in Germany—the hippies of the twenties.

The van bounces my thoughts back to the present again. Hermann tells us that a few weeks ago he and Hans Meier participated in a big peace demonstration in Philadelphia. They represented the bruderhof at the celebration of the three hundredth anniversary of the arrival of the first German immigrants in America. The two members of the bruderhof, 82 and 69 years of age, seemed to have felt happy among the young people as they carried the bruderhof's banner for peace.

The road winds its way beneath Interstate 87. On the

left a river appears with an old covered bridge.

"We're almost there," says Danni. Ahead we can see on the right a wooden oval sign which points to the bruderhof. "Hutterian Brethren," it says at the top, with "Woodcrest Bruderhof" and "Makers of Community Playthings" added below. The big sign is firmly fastened to two strong posts.

Here we are! Now we're in for it, I think. But so far everything is peaceful. The well-surfaced private drive winds up the wooded hill. Then in the middle of the road appears a stop sign. On the left I notice some large workshops and warehouses—the "shop" (the factory of Community Playthings) from which the brothers and sisters make their living.

We bear right up a steep incline. Danni blows the horn "because of the children, you know," and once again we turn sharply to the right. In front of us is a large garage, with a number of cars parked around it. Now we can see the many imposing houses of the village which actually make up the bruderhof.

Before I can adjust to the situation, we have already passed the barrier that leads to the housing area of the village. Slowly our minibus rolls up the gentle incline of the road, beneath old, gigantic maple trees. To the right and to the left the luscious green lawns are suddenly alive with people young and old, big and small, coming to meet us in colored shirts and broad suspenders crossed at the back, waving polka-dotted kerchieves as they accompany our car. Ahead of us a few children sit on the lawn, playing with three white rabbits. They wave happily and we wave back. On the right we pass a venerable graybeard and on the left a man wearing a black jacket and a straw hat.

Hands reach into the open window. "Hello!" and "Thank you," we say. "Welcome, welcome!" they reply. We stop. The door of our car opens and an elderly, smiling, gray-haired woman, who wants to ride along with us, climbs in.

"Hello, welcome! I'm Winifred. It's good you've come," she greets us in German with a jolly English accent. Winifred, we learn later is one of the "housemothers" and, among other things, works in the quite impressive archives of the bruderhof.

At the next curve we finally alight and in no time are surrounded.

"Welcome, I'm Ed. I'm Marilyn. Welcome! I'm Dick. Greetings."

The lawns are teeming with Jonathans, Dons, Christophers, Susannas, Dorlises, Kathys, Joannas, Peters. How can I remember all these names? Especially since the way they dress makes everyone look almost alike.

Surrounding us are 134 cheap-rimmed glasses, 117 kerchieves, 197 pairs of sneakers, 122 crumpled jeans, and 78 colored little bonnets. Is this a bruderhof? It seems more like a poultry yard!

At any rate, for the next few minutes we are occupied with shaking hands, groping for English words, smiling. So many are glad we've come. One hardly knows what to do with so much joy, let alone how to react to it. Perhaps they are so friendly because we have come from "good old Germany." Or else that is how people are in America— friendly, relaxed, and a bit superficial. But actually, all this looks quite genuine.

Perhaps they really mean it seriously and simply are like that at the bruderhof.

By the time we get happily back into our van, I have pressed the hands of about three generations of Arnolds, two generations of Moodys, Swingers, and Stängls—and others I have already forgotten.

The last stretch we could actually have walked—except, of course, for our baggage. The road goes up a hill, down the other side, and around a few bends. Then we stand in front of the house in which we shall spend the next few weeks. Quite a big box it is, at least three stories high, built right into the hillside. On all four corners stand large green trees. Many lovely flowers are planted all around. I can't help myself, but it really looks like a home for pensioned hippies—really quite unique!

Behind the house you can see the great wooded plain of this part of New York and, beyond that, the romantic backdrop of the Catskill Mountains emerging through the haze. At the entrance again many persons in polka-dotted kerchieves and crossed suspenders stand ready to welcome us. The children, the colors, the sun, the trees, the whole landscape before us seems unreal. If from behind a bush a lion would appear, with children riding on its back, and a snake would glide down from a tree, I truly would believe that I had arrived in Paradise. Or perhaps, since we are in America, in Walt Disney's *Snow White and the Seven Dwarfs* with me in the movie!

Of course there are neither dwarfs nor lions here (but snakes, as we shall find out later)—nothing but friendly people, and a very hospitable home.

So then—let's go in! As I open the door I see on my right a thermometer. It reads 102 degrees! Just as I thought—it's as hot as I feel. Of course it's 102 degrees Fahrenheit, which is 36 degrees Centigrade. But with humidity such as this, one could just as well call it 102 degrees Centigrade.

Behind the front door there seems to be a central wardrobe for this floor. At least 23 raincoats and 18 pairs of rubber boots, like me, are just waiting for a refreshing downpour of rain!

The house in which we live seems to be one of the newest. It was built by the people themselves. They have their own architect and a building crew which is kept busy with one construction project or another. The bruderhof is growing. The house we live in with its friendly colors and much wood paneling is comfortable. It is also ingeniously constructed for special bruderhof purposes. Around a central rectangular light and air well are bathrooms and a small open kitchen. A hallway connects all the apartments, with living rooms and bedrooms arranged along the outside of the house. In order not to disturb one another unduly, the house is built on two levels, rather than with one continuous floor.

Did you understand that? No? Well, if you enter the house and go up half a staircase, you reach the Domers with their eight children and whoever else lives there. And that is the first floor—level A, on the left side of the house. Now if you go up half a staircase again, you reach Carroll and Doris King with their thirteen children. (And there, in the morning you might see a huge breakfast table!) Well, in any case, this is the first floor, level B, on the right half of the house. If you then go up another half staircase, you reach the level where evidently we are now going to live.

"Joyful welcome, Uli and Christel" is written on a large sign on the door—and many flowers are painted all around it. The third-graders did this, the class of the eight-year-olds in the school here.

After witnessing our initial enjoyment of the big pleasant room, the cut flowers, the 23 greeting cards, the four jars of homemade jam, the freshly made candy, and the gorgeous view through the window, our hosts politely leave the room. Now one can close the door, stand with one's back to the big double bed, close one's eyes, and . . . wait a moment! First switch on the big antique fan. Ah, that feels good. . . . Then plop down, breathe deeply, and for a long time do nothing at all!

"Well—I really had not expected such a reception!" I exclaim after a while. Christel and I feel quite done in and surprised. "My, that was like an official state welcome!" But not only the friendly welcome fascinates me. I am impressed with the harmony and festive atmosphere which one feels here. Everything fits nicely together—the people, the colorful flowers, the friendliness, the radiant sun and the blue sky, the happy faces, the houses, and the landscape.

In my first euphoria I think that I could imagine heaven being like this—at least a small heaven. Or one could perhaps compare the atmosphere here with a holiday camp, where old and young vacation together—only this experience extends over thirty years!

I recall again the anxieties I had because of Holzach's book, of his stern and rather gray picture of the Hutterites. No, they really do not seem to be like that. And yet the three American Society of Brothers communities and the one in Darvell, England, have belonged to the Hutterian Brethren group again since 1974. This ancient community of faith was founded by the radical Tirolian Christian Jacob Hutter in the sixteenth century. So actually genuine Hutterites live in these joyful bruderhofs. These people live together in community of goods like the early Christians. They abstain from military service because they are absolute pacifists.

Their affiliation with the old Hutterites is quite apparent in their dress, especially among the women. One can see this readily. They wear the familiar black kerchieves with white spots, which in America are called "polka dots," and long print skirts all cut to the same pattern, with a vest and usually a white blouse. Their dress doesn't look exactly like the latest fashion, but the variety of colors and materials make it pleasing to the eyes. Hutterish—but also a bit like the youth movement.

Even the children dress differently. All girls from babyhood on wear a kind of bonnet. Mostly they look really nice—made in strong reds, greens, yellows, and blues— happy and childlike. The Hutterian women and girls have mastered the art of braiding the hair. Their hair is not worn loose. The younger ones have braids—and the older ones buns, or whatever one calls what is concealed under the kerchief.

In this matter the bruderhof men have it easier. Certainly they do not wear the latest "hit" from Woolworth's, although their sturdy trousers and brightly colored shirts look quite normal. The first thing that we notice is the apparently obligatory use of suspenders for the pants. Possibly these are even necessary because of the way the pants are cut. At any rate in this rural area the men stand a better chance of not being recognized immediately as Woodcresters. But obviously the costume theme is not so important for the bruderhofers as for the interested visitors.

The necessary changes in garb after uniting with the Hutterians again in 1974 were not easy for many. But meanwhile they have grown accustomed to it and enjoy the beautiful picture the men make in their Sunday suits when they sit spic and span in formation with their bright blue shirts. And on occasional visits, beyond the protecting borders of the bruderhof, they are not ashamed of the way they dress.

For the bruderhof teenagers, however, contact with the "world" is intensive and continuous. No later than the age of fourteen they go to Kingston High School, six miles away.

Perhaps it becomes clear to them there that the majority of American youths have little interest in wearing a standard costume—although the other high schoolers certainly have fads and fashions that dictate to a remarkable extent how they dress. With fashion one is lost in the crowd; in costume one stands out. The "Woodies" are neither narrow-minded nor very different from other teenagers their own age. Routinely the bruderhof children stand at the top of the class in their respective courses. In a recent year eight of the 700 local students were honored and awarded scholarships for special achievement at the graduation celebration. Six of the eight children came from the bruderhof. This is not unusual.

I look at the clock. It is time to start getting ready. To my relief I have found out that one can lie comfortably on a bruderhof bed, and no doubt also sleep well. The beds are also produced here. We seem to have the standard model—a little hard perhaps, but healthy. At the head of the bed I discover a row of books on a shelf—Plough Books, naturally, including Eberhard Arnold, in a variety of colors, sizes, and editions. These are put together in their own printshop and book bindery and distributed through

the bruderhof publishing house—"Plough Publishing."
They include interesting lectures, sometimes difficult to
read and digest. Arnold did not write exactly for the
average man on the street. Already in the twenties he was
well known for his powerful original language.

We are invited by Rudi and Winifred for supper. Danni
will meet us and take us to the Darvell house. We don't
know our way around the village yet and have no idea who
lives where. Even in our house here, "Sunnyside," over
sixty people live. Other houses are named after former bruderhofs: "Primavera," "Oaksey," "Alm," and "Forest
River."

Rudi and Winifred are our "guest parents" for the duration of our stay. We may turn especially to them with all
our questions and problems. After we arrive at the Darvell
house, we learn that we will be eating outside. It is a beautiful summer evening. Each house has two or three picnic
places with grills and benches, and often an old split-open
oil barrel for grilling meat near the front of the house.

It is Wednesday, a family evening in the bruderhof
schedule, when they eat in small groups. At the most, a few
guests are invited, a neighbor from down the hall or an
older single brother. We are not the only ones who are eating outside this evening. Around us at different picnic
places small groups are sitting together, under trees, next to
a rose garden, and on the grassy slopes. From the right side
a song drifts over to us, from the left spicy smoke from a
grill fire. The well-spread table shows a European choice of
foods. There is noodle salad, Russian eggs, bread, and tea. I
am relieved that the bruderhof is not yet infected by the
McDonald's food culture.

Hermann, our faithful protecter in all unfamiliar situations and questions of bruderhof behavior, is sitting with us at the table. According to bruderhof custom supper begins with a song—in German, of course. This is not because German guests happen to be sitting at the supper table, but rather because at least half of their voluminous treasury of songs are German in origin. To be sure, most of them have been translated into English, and often the German version is sung followed by the English one. The singing is beautiful. One could devote a special chapter (together with a tape recording) to the wonderful four-part singing of the bruderhof.

At any rate we also begin to sing: "As the far-flung stars are circling . . . ." I feel a bit self-conscious as I join in lustily. Naturally, one must show that one wishes to take part. Kalle, a reluctant singer, receives a mildly critical side glance from Hermann. Kalle reacts guiltily. Like a schoolboy caught in the act he begins to sing with us timidly and unsteadily. Having seen the whole thing, I start to laugh in the middle of the song, but just manage to suppress it. I am not yet sure about how much one is allowed to laugh at the bruderhof. Kalle (or "Kaaarrl" as the bruderhofers call him since hearing that his name is actually Karl Hermann) perhaps does not know the old evening song which was just suggested.

Rudi and Winifred turn out to be very pleasant and fine people. Rudi came to the Rhön bruderhof as a seven-year-old orphan and has remained to this day. In the thirties, the taking in, care, and support of homeless children was one of the bruderhof areas of work until this activity was forbidden by the National Socialists in 1933. Later Rudi learned to know Winifred on the Cotswold bruderhof to which the bruderhofers had been obliged to emigrate in 1937.

Gradually I became accustomed to the fact that every conversation at the bruderhof is surrounded by a living inventory of bruderhof history. It is possible to talk with people, and then to go to the archives and read about their childhood and youth. Most bruderhofers have become well acquainted with their history through these records.

Rudi is the building coordinator for the bruderhof. But today he tells about the bruderhof prison work which he helps with in his spare time. Several times a week groups of brothers go to the neighboring prisons, sing with inmates, read to them from the Bible, and have discussions—for example about pacifism. Lively talks follow what the Bible really teaches.

Later our conversation turns to the difficult time the bruderhof faced in Paraguay. But their reports are remarkably general and thin. In some way this seems to be a sore point in their history. The subject of Paraguay for many bruderhofers is at least as untapped as that distant and hot South American country was in 1941 when they arrived there. Naturally that makes me all the more curious, and I decide to dig deeper into this area.

It is already getting dark as we set out for a short evening walk. We head in a southerly direction and come quickly to the fields and surrounding woods. We are still meeting people with whom we apparently have not yet shaken hands. It is a pity that the majority of bruderhofers wear these ugly black-rimmed hospital glasses which in the fifties were perhaps the height of fashion, though even then they couldn't have looked pleasing. I am especially disturbed by this since one meets so many interesting and expressive faces which are totally dominated by these dark monstrosities on the nose. Why are the bruderhofers so reluctant to acknowledge human beauty?

As we walk, I reflect again on the quiet harmony of life in this community. Everything looks beautiful and in order. For instance in a room the lamps, pictures, and furniture are in keeping with one another. I ask myself whether that should not also be true with people. According to the Bible, men and women are the crown of creation. For them to live together in a tasteful and orderly way has nothing to do with the lust of the eyes or with the pride of life, but rather with beauty and harmony in which I cannot discover anything sinful.

People are just coming back from the swimming pool which they themselves dammed up and which is five minutes away from the bruderhof. Children with wet hair in strands and shining happy eyes walk with their swim bags in their hands. They say hello. They pause to chat. It's a summer evening straight out of a folksong book or a Ludwig Richter drawing. Fireflies sail through the mild evening air. The cicadas and other grasshoppers no longer sing, but emit a beastly loud screech. I hope I can sleep with that going on.

But sleep comes quicker than I thought. Half-conscious, I am aware that I am beginning to dream. I sit in the time machine I once saw in a movie and turn the dial back. My goal is Germany in the twenties. Gradually time rewinds past me. I see spotted kerchieves, long skirts, children, rabbits, and flowers. Faster and faster the pictures fly past my eyes. I see blazing flames and youth with torches; wandering songs ring out and young couples in simple peasant dress leap through the flames of a campfire. Really, this is how it used to be. Suddenly the serious eyes of Eberhard Arnold appear out of the mist. His face with the round academic glasses grows dim and disappears.

Now young girls in white dresses and flower garlands rush past, hands clasped for a circle dance. I see the framework of an old bruderhof, the meeting hall, the grounds, and an old draw well. I can hear it all quite clearly now. It must have been just like this in Germany at that time. A night watchman is singing. I can hear his voice: "Hear, good folk! Now dark is heaven, for the clock has struck eleven. . . ."

But stop! Something's not right. Astonished, I sit up in bed. The night watchman is singing in English! And it isn't a dream. I am not in Germany in the twenties. I am in Woodcrest, USA, in 1984, and this night watchman is real!

"Hey, Christel, listen! There is a night watchman, and he is singing the German night watchman's song—only in English!" We jump out of bed and look out of the window. It's true. There stands a young man with a flashlight and a huge sheepdog—a real, genuine, live night watchman!

"Wow! When we tell them this at home, no one will believe us," I whisper to Christel. If someone had seen me later that night, in my watchman-protected sleep, perhaps they would have noticed the bliss of childhood on my face. . . .

4

The "Moondance" Solution

Breakfast with the Meier family begins punctually at 7:15 a.m. The living room table fills up with fifteen people—one grandma, two parents, nine Meier children, and three guests. We are served coffee, eggs, toast, and homemade jams, as well as white clover honey. The honey is from an old Hutterian bruderhof in Manitoba, which specializes in beekeeping. It owns over a thousand beehives on specially cultivated clover fields. (There is a kind of domestic economy between bruderhofs. One supplies honey; the other delivers chairs in exchange.)

The room in which we are sitting could just as well belong to another Hutterian house or another bruderhof. The basic furnishings include a simple upholstered couch, a quite large expandable table, chairs, and a rocking chair. There is also a counter which holds all kinds of crockery together with a two-burner gas cooker (something like the breakfast-coffee appliance) in every self-contained apartment. A bookshelf with some Plough volumes and a selection of songbooks is also a standard part of the decor. The living-room-kitchen-dayrooms are finished in strong friendly colors. On the walls hang home-painted pictures by the artistically gifted brothers and sisters of the bruderhof. The pictures are also joyfully colorful, with some of the realism of the German youth movement.

The family quarters differ for the most part only in small details. One family has a beautiful old clock standing in the corner, while another has an aquarium bubbling on a chest of drawers. A third one has an old upholstered armchair. But in general the rooms glow with usefulness and simplicity, nothing overdone or showy. Care is taken not to provoke envy in others.

The fact that Danni still prefers maté (a kind of green tea, the national drink of South America), is evidence that he grew up at the bruderhof in Paraguay. Danni spent some years separated from the community. He experienced hard things. For a year, he transported timber on the tropical rivers of Paraguay. Today he is happy to have found his way back to the community.

Life in the Paraguay bruderhof was difficult. "Many children died," Danni remembers. "We were hungry. Again and again there were plagues of locusts. Pesky caterpillars had to be pulled off the vegetables. And the nights were cold, sometimes below freezing."

At 7:50 the small children disperse, accompanied by an older sister. They head for the kindergarten or preschool where, apart from the midday pause, they spend the whole day in their age-groups. The rest of the table circle soon breaks up also. At eight o'clock Danni starts work in the metal shop. Rose Marie, his wife, will clear up at home till nine o'clock. Then like all the other women, she will go to her currently assigned place of work. Hermann stops by to lead us on a big tour of the bruderhof.

We have hardly started when we meet Manuel who, it turns out, is one of the two nightwatchmen. He did the second shift from 2:00 to 6:00 a.m., and looks quite tired.

"Do you really sing the nightwatchman's song every hour?" I ask him, adding that we heard his colleague earlier in the night and enjoyed him immensely.

"Yes, we sing at each hour between ten o'clock in the evening and four o'clock in the morning," he replies. "We have many old and sick brothers and sisters who cannot sleep some nights. For them it is comforting and reassuring to hear that someone is always awake." I understand. This is no old-fashioned German custom, but another conscious way of sharing in each other's lives here and now.

We pass a little house with white wooden walls, a pyramid-shaped slate roof, and a small tower on the top. It appears to be a remnant of the old houses built by the former owner, a textile manufacturer whose factory down in the valley is now covered over by the dammed-up lake. He sold this property with his splendid house and the surrounding buildings to the bruderhof in the fifties.

"This building was once the icehouse," Hermann explains. "It had terrifically thick, insulated walls. It was filled with ice blocks in the winter, which the factory workers had to saw out of the frozen river and drag up here. In the icehouse the blocks remained frozen till autumn. Today our young unmarried men live here."

That makes sense, I think. An icehouse for the youths. How appropriate. In an icehouse wrong thoughts will certainly not flourish. But the bruderhofers appear not to joke about the matter in this way. Instead they refer to the "nice-house"—and that is clever also.

Our first aim this morning is to see the two new large houses in the middle of the village. They are especially striking because of their large covered verandas, at least fifteen feet wide, which are now used as a parking place for all kinds of vehicles. Dozens of scooters, tricycles, and wagons are standing in orderly rows. Later in the day these verandas will be full of playing children. Even when it is raining the children can benefit from the fresh air.

To the right of the bruderhof main path lies the "babyhouse" for the tiny ones. To our left is the big children's house, surrounded by an enormous lawn with all kinds of play equipment produced by the bruderhofs. The communities manufacture kindergarten items and children's toys as a major part of their livelihood. Perhaps this lawn is not so much a section of the children's house as "Test-place No. 1" of the development section of Community Playthings (their trade name). Whatever the case, the children thrive in this environment.

When one sees the lavish and well-equipped house for the bruderhof children, it becomes quickly clear how much importance is ascribed to the education and care of the smallest residents. Nevertheless, to eyes accustomed to small families, these houses are at first something of a shock. In the babyhouse five cots stand side-by-side with sleeping babies in them, arranged according to age. Already these infants are becoming accustomed to community. Over each cot hangs a hand-painted plaque with the name of the baby. The care—for the most part by young bruderhof sisters—is thorough and individualized. Even so, it seems to me a little like a warehouse for newborn children, a strict, highly organized institution.

The women entrusted with the care of the babies seem

to take their work seriously and are very loving and responsible with the little ones. The system has its advantages. The single and childless bruderhof women like to spend time with the children. On the other hand, the parents are glad at times to be free so that both can devote themselves to the work of the community. Thus a number of typical community problems are solved at the same time and in a harmonious and profitable way for all concerned.

The kindergarten which we visit next seems more normal to me. Surrounded by the typical bright-colored bruderhof equipment, the children are arranged in circles by age-groups. There are seven "Onies" in one group, five "Twosies," eight "Threesies," and so on. One group is on its way to a small pool for swimming. Others with push toys are on a sightseeing tour through the village. A third group is with the pony wagon in the woods. The fourth sits before us eating a snack or "second breakfast." Special half-round, bow-shaped tables are standing everywhere, an invention of Community Playthings. Up to eight children sit on the outer rim. The woman in charge sits at the inner curve, where she can see and reach all the children.

The parents are responsible for the education of their children. But because father and mother must also do for their share of communal work, the children are looked after in their age-groups between 8:00 a.m. and 2:00 p.m., and between 3:00 p.m. and 5:30 p.m. Usually they also eat by age-groups at midday and in the evening. The relationship to the group sister or teacher becomes very strong. This does not seem to pose a problem for the families, though. Because those who care for the children are members of the community, they enjoy the complete trust of the parents. In any case, parents are working not far away.

Nursing mothers can interrupt their work to feed their babies. When other problems arise, the parents are soon on the scene.

At any rate, bruderhof children are less bound to their parents than those of "normal" families. Visitors sometimes have difficulty in adjusting to this idea. But the life of the bruderhof as a community is possible only through this kind of intensive care of the children. Otherwise, young mothers would be excluded from many community experiences through the burden of caring for their little children.

I recall some German experiments of living together. In them the young mothers are hampered because of their children. Willingly or unwillingly, they forego the long group discussions and communal undertakings, and thus are not able to take part fully in the community activities. It is different here. Community in the bruderhof is for everyone. The women are not at a disadvantage. They are not required to forego community to make community life possible. The pattern of education at the bruderhofs helps maintain a practical balance in the involvements of husbands and wives, a fact which obviously works out positively for the community in many ways.

Because of the type of education they experience, Bruderhof children from the earliest years develop a special relationship to groups and community. Problems of the "only child" are not to be found here. The relationship to their own age-group is enormously strong, possibly as strong as to the parents. Fritzy Muller [i.e. Tom, Dick, or Harry] beginning at six weeks of age spends eight hours or more of each day with the same boys and girls his age. This continues until college age. Bruderhof children do not experience many of the problems of those growing up in a small family. The children relate more easily with other youngsters their age. Sharing is not quite so difficult as is often true of children on the outside.

At this point a caution flag goes up in my mind. Does the bruderhof education system produce only uniform, boring, and unoriginal little bruderhof people, a gray sameness? I am too little of an educator to be able to judge adequately the theoretical aspects of this question. But my observations seem to run in the opposite direction. Seldom have I seen so many open, individual, and original children as here. Bruderhof children impress me as unusually lively, curious, confident, and relaxed. They are real children. Nothing false, no grown-up affectedness, has as yet crept in. They are attractively innocent, as children should be, in contrast to those in many small families on the outside. Without doubt, the bruderhof children are perhaps the strongest and most convincing advertisement for the bruderhof way of life, and perhaps the community's greatest treasure.

I cannot argue with the result of the bruderhof education. But the rather stiff, regimented, and strict way they go about it continues to perplex me. The narrow, regulated, ordered pattern is somewhat distasteful to me, but the naturalness and open purity of the children themselves are very attractive. Perhaps this apparent contradiction can be explained through the bruderhof's writings. Eberhard Arnold defined the approach in his book, *Children's Education in Community*.

He called for "reverence, childlike prayer, self-discipline, freedom to dare, love and truthfulness, freedom from possessiveness, purity, childlikeness, and sympathy for poverty and suffering." This goal in education should not be reached in a one-sided, intellectual manner, but by a comprehensive and close-to-nature approach.

The key to achieving this high demand is that only trustworthy teachers and educators, fully in agreement with the goal of the bruderhof, are given responsibility for the children. The decisive element is certainly a spiritual one. Bruderhof teachers are not merely "convinced," "interested," or "hired" educators. They are spiritual fathers and mothers who really love the children entrusted to them. Love—that is the context in which the meticulously ordered and strict-sounding educational theory of the bruderhof produces pure, unspoiled, and happy children.

Naturally, bruderhof people also have their weaknesses and make their share of mistakes. They experience failures, problems, and difficulties. But the mistakes of a secular professional teacher influenced by worldly connections will not be made here.

After touring the children's house, we move on to the preschool, which is situated in the school building, the largest house on the bruderhof. Like the older students in the eight grades of the bruderhof school, the children are elsewhere. It is still summer vacation time. They are all doing special work, projects, paddling canoes on the lake down by the river, or picking wild strawberries for making jam. The new school year will start next Sunday with a celebration for those entering the first grade.

On the lower level of the schoolhouse, a bookbinding department is set up. It is managed by an 82-year-old bookbinder from Breslau. He seems to be a genuine old-world craftsman.

Next we go to the laundry, a work area completely in charge of the women. Kathy shows me with pride her "big baby," a monstrous washing machine, more than six by six feet large, and positioned on huge metal shock absorbers, truly a community-size appliance.

Every family here is assigned a certain washday in the week. They bring their various kinds of clothing in separate net bags (to avoid mixing and losing items) and they are washed right away. We were astonished to discover that they have a chemist in the community who, using an appropriate formula, is able to make bulk quantities of detergent, water softener, hair shampoo, and soap. "That is a much cheaper way," says Kathy. "City people are exploited by such things as brand-name shampoos or cosmetics, which are actually quite simple to make."

In addition, just now, clothing is being washed for Uganda in Africa. The community has chartered a container, which in the course of the week will be filled with relief goods. The youngsters are making penholders for children in Uganda. The women in the sewing rooms are not running the twenty machines to make their own clothing this week. They are sewing garments for Africa.

The attempt to live as self-sufficiently as possible is not limited to water softeners. The bruderhof has its own waterworks with a reservoir and a number of wells. Most of the buildings of the bruderhof, together with electrical installations, they have constructed and wired themselves. They have a filling station to service their own vehicles. They grow most of their produce in their own fields which pays for itself. (Potatoes are somewhat cheaper when bought.)

Self-sufficiency has also been achieved in the

professions. The bruderhof has its own optician, several doctors and nurses, its own teachers (as we have already noted), and even a surveyor who has just completed his training. Some time ago the Deer Spring bruderhof bought a hill covered with woodland. (When oil becomes expensive again, they will be able to heat with their own felled timber.) That required the services of a surveyor. The continual changing, enlarging, and building of new houses also demands trained personnel.

Our tour moves next to the facilities of the bruderhof chemist, who has developed formulas for making soap and cleaning supplies. His laboratory rooms over the factory area look highly technical. Sacks of raw materials and barrels of finished products stand scattered about. Arranged on the worktables are flasks with colored liquids, test tubes, and rubber gloves. A converted cement mixer serves as a chemical mixer, and a self-made dispenser for shampoo stands nearby.

"Most things are cheaper when produced here," the enterprising chemist tells us. "Many cleaning products are more than 90 percent water. The shampoo we make costs us 20 cents for the same quantity you pay at least five dollars for in the city." He calls his floor cleaner "Moon-dance" (in place of "Sundance" at the supermarket). Then there is "Amber," a dish-washing liquid; "Terget," for the rinsing machine; "Enzate" for Kathy's "big baby"; and "Solvit," a hand cleaner. With over one thousand bruderhofers in the three Eastern United States communities, it is certainly possible to save quite a bit!

But the community's self-sufficiency extends even further. Some time ago two gifted technicians in the workshop decided to produce their own source of power. The many wood shavings wasted in the production of Community Playthings could be used to make electricity, they decided. For turning the wood shavings into gas, they built an experimental installation, the somewhat rusted remains of which are still to be seen down in the shop. Anyhow, they succeeded in driving an old 40 horsepower Volkswagen motor with wood gas. Coupled with a generator this actually produced current. But the whole project required too much work and was often in need of repair, so they gave it up.

Perhaps the wind could be harnessed to produce energy! The school received the task of making preliminary inquiries and recording the possible use of wind currents. Teachers and pupils consulted with metal specialists. They built a 60-foot-high aluminum mast which, with a measuring implement, was erected at the highest point on the bruderhof. Exciting and interesting as the project was for the schoolchildren, producing electricity for the community with a windmill did not prove practical. For a year, the measurements showed an average wind speed of only nine miles an hour, much too slow to produce a reliable source of current.

However, another school project functions well each spring. Surrounded by the tall trunks of maple trees between the shop and village stands the "maple-sap factory." This is a large open wooden shed which has an oversized stovepipe and a pan twelve feet square. Every February and March a fierce fire burns under this pan.

The schoolchildren collect the sap from the maples as the trees awaken from their winter sleep. This is a time of great fun for all involved, a festive occasion for the whole community.

A hole is bored in the tree and a tube inserted, under which a bucket is hung. The children collect the maple sap and pour it into large tanks. This is fed into the pan where the water evaporates and the sap thickens into maple syrup. In America this highly valued product is eaten with most anything and is practically as important as catsup! Homemade maple syrup is sold in the display room of Community Playthings and at a bruderhof stand on the highway. The proceeds go to a relief organization as a gift from the children. This is also wholesome education.

When one enters the main administration office of the bruderhof's Community Playthings and Rifton Equipment for the Handicapped firm, it becomes quite clear that the bruderhof is not a folklorish museum piece out of the twenties. Alongside many young community girls, their colleague "Willy" is at work—the only one in the office who does not appear in costume. Willy's surname is "Wang"—Willy Wang, the bruderhof computer. He assists with the general bookkeeping, inventory control, order entry, and whatever else is suitable work for a computer. At the moment there is no other way to manage the adminstration of the bruderhof business without Willy.

The kindergarten tables, building bricks, tricycles, wheelchairs, climbing frames, and other sturdy products are offered in two colorful catalogs. Although the prices are not cheap, business flourishes.

The community produces high-quality goods, exchanging without hesitation any faulty article within a year, and beyond that providing necessary repairs. Over 100,000 color catalogs are mailed to customers every year, spreading the good reputation of the bruderhof far and wide. There is hardly a country in the world from which orders have not come. There are even shipments to Saudi Arabia. At the moment there are more orders coming in than they can supply. But in the brotherhood meeting the communities have agreed not to work overtime. Work should not dominate their life. Their work is a service project. The goal is not to gain as much profit as possible.

The bruderhofers are somewhat more broadminded in their policy with their customers. One of the largest sources of orders is the U.S. Army. In spite of the bruderhof's firm pacifism, they fill these orders. Perhaps they are glad for every dollar they can pull from the Army's pocket in this way. Whatever money is used for kindergarten furniture will not be spent on bombs and rockets, the clever bruderhofers seem to think. Perhaps they have discovered a new method of turning swords into plowshares.

Now we hear the ringing of the great community bell. It is 12:15 p.m., time for dinner. Together with all the shop brothers we head for the Rhönhouse, the large central dininghall which has the same name on all four bruderhofs.

Eberhard Arnold said: "The daily mealtimes should take on the character of a consecrated feast." Well, we shall see. . . .

5

No Law but Love

About 250 bruderhofers stream with us toward the dining room, approaching from all directions in a starlike formation. Twice a day the dining room is the festive focal point of the community. A wooden ceiling with heavy beams arches over the large octangular hall. The walls are painted a powerful blue, with large 6 x 9-foot pictures hanging on them.

The pictures are changed frequently: scenes of young people bearing torches in the Rhön Mountains, a view of the hilly land surrounding the Rhön bruderhof, the forest spring near the old Sannerz House—all painted by artistically gifted bruderhofers.

On the left side of the hall is a large stage. At the front of the room a row of windows offers a generous and romantic view of the Catskill Mountains. At suppertime, everyone is treated to a magnificent sunset, resplendent with all its varied colors.

Over the doorway to the kitchen hang three clocks: the first shows Woodcrest time—12:30; the second reads 5:30

p.m., the time at the English bruderhof in Darvell; and the third says 11:30 a.m., the time at the old Hutterite sister colonies in Manitoba and South Dakota.

We are a little late, for most of the 250 set places are already taken. It is a truly festive, expectant, colorful picture—but also a little frightening, standing before such a gathered crowd of bruderhofers.

As soon as all are seated, the two doors are closed. A crackling sound comes over the large loudspeaker, and through the air (kept moving by four large ventilator fans in the ceiling) Dick Domer's vigorous voice rings out, "Is New Meadow Run on the line?"

Following more crackles and rustles, the answer comes. "Yes, Dick, we greet you very warmly!"

"And Deer Spring?"

"Yes, Dick, we can hear you!"

The three U.S. communities are now connected with one another over a telephone network which is permanently rented.

Dick suggests a song, and a few seconds later all three groups are "singing in" the midday meal together. And how they sing! There is no comparison with the often thin, sometimes painfully dragging church singing with which I am familiar. The four-part harmony rings so full and fresh that no instrumental accompaniment is needed. It becomes clear through the powerful intensity of the singing how many young and middle-aged members this bruderhof has in it.

Singing is taken very seriously here for its spiritual content. Often a general atmosphere which cannot immediately be put into words is given in a suitably chosen song which expresses the feelings of all. The communities are cautious about big spiritual words and empty theological talk.

Many of the bruderhofers come from churches in which pious words are used but in which the corresponding deeds and life are lacking. Here they tend to say, "We don't want to talk. We want to live, to do, to act." But often a simple song moves the bruderhofers deeply, expressing words of prayer, thankfulness, praise, and joy.

The actual meal begins with a short silence after the song. There is no public saying of grace. They do not want to put pressure on persons with commonly used words, but all should be free to fill the silence with something fitting for themselves. They would rather be honest than appear superficially pious.°

Personally, I am not quite satisfied with this solution. Certainly it is good to be genuine. But the general reserve in spoken prayer seems to me to be an institutionalized overreaction. They have countered a swing to the right (too much empty talk) with a swing to the left (undue verbal restraint). If a meaningful middle way is not found, the next generation may adopt a pious tradition which does not express the ideal position but is rather a reaction to the present practice.

It seems to me it is better to confront too many words with the right words rather than with too few words. But the bruderhof life is constantly flowing. That which is accepted today may be modified tomorrow. Today's problems are often soon forgotten.

For the midday meal today we are served rice with meat

° Since this was written, the practice has changed. Usually now the prayer is audible.

Emmy and Eberhard Arnold as a young couple.

The Rhön bruderhof, the community's home from 1926 to 1937.

Welcome to Woodcrest.

Hidden in the woods, a part of the Woodcrest bruderhof.

Little Red Riding Hoods on a school outing.

The best of care for the youngest persons in the community.

Fresh air and a tour of the grounds.

Concentration in "bruderhof blue."

Playmates.

Tomato harvest.

School recess time.

Enjoying a meal together.

The kindergarten moves into the schoolhouse.

What shall we do next?

Oh, dear, where was it again?

Daddy is our teacher.

12:30—dinnertime!

Summer vacation.

72

sauce and fresh vegetables. In addition, there is milk for the children to drink and ice water for the grown-ups. Durable plastic cups and plates are used. With so many children, this cuts down on breakage.

Rotating teams of waiters serve the meal, distribute seconds, and afterward do the enormous dishwashing duty. Specially trained women and young girls do the cooking. A remarkable distribution of work "a la bruderhof"!

At midday and evening, warm meals are served. The food is usually simple but tasty, and prepared with care. Today for dessert there are oranges, some of which are slightly bad. Perhaps the steward (or *Weinzedel*, as the old Hutterians call him) has obtained a whole truckload cheap. They were too ripe to sell for the market. The bruderhof takes good advantage of such opportunities.

When the electricity fails in the neighboring supermarket, the bruderhof truck is on the spot. When the wholesale fruit dealer wants to get rid of a load of overripe bananas, the bruderhof has enough hands to sort them and enough hungry mouths to eat them. Other foods are purchased in bulk just before their specified expiration dates. With their own truck, which transports partly finished products from the other bruderhofs to the Woodcrest workshop, they go off for a load of overripe tomatoes, still usable fruit juices, and a profitable wholesale purchase of wieners. One can live well and cheaply in a community, although eating oranges or tomatoes in every imaginable form for two consecutive weeks may become a bit tiresome.

Except for the small children, those responsible for them, and individual old people or sick ones, everyone takes part in the community mealtimes. But those who are absent can listen in their own homes and follow what is happening in the dining room over a loudspeaker. Everyone is included—to achieve true community, to form a unity. These are the reasons for employing the expensive technology which makes it possible over a distance of 400 miles (that's how far New Meadow Run in western Pennsylvania is from Woodcrest).

But singing is not the most important reason for the electronic hookup between the communities and those who cannot be present at the dining hall. There is also a sharing of experiences and thoughts. Something may be read aloud from Eberhard Arnold or from other books of a worthwhile nature. Sometimes the latest news items with their background are shared. Sometimes brothers or sisters who have just returned from visiting the English bruderhof or who were in Germany give a report of their journey.

Also guests may be asked to tell about their work, and about their thoughts and purposes. So in the community there is no lack of information. Each one hears what is shared with the group. The same themes and subjects concern the whole community. There is much to think over communally.

The connection with the other two American bruderhofs is not arranged for every mealtime. The conference call is used only when something important and of interest to all is being reported.

These outer forms and arrangements are an expression of an important theological concern of the bruderhof. The main thing for them is unity, harmonious agreement, and oneness. And that should be not only in the big things but also in the small everyday things. They want to experience a communal development, with no single bruderhof having too much life of its own. Even when they live in separate places, they want to be a united community. Outward unity is only the expression of a much deeper inner union.

This ideal also has historical roots. Eberhard Arnold said:

> It is terrible that in so-called Christianity they are so disunited, not only in the different churches, but also among those who earnestly want to be Christians. But it is absolutely no help to remain silent over all the questions where there is disunity.

For this reason, at brotherhood meetings lively discussion takes place to find the right way on a particular issue at a particular time. In the end the decision is not democratic, but through consensus. The majority vote does not determine the way, but unity does. Unity is only reached when each one agrees from the heart. Only then can the way be followed together. At the same time it is possible for one person to hold a different conviction from the rest of the community. If so, the decision has to be postponed. Other talks follow. In the end the point of view of the one member may be acted upon.

> A conviction in unanimity can only take place on the basis of frankness, freewillingness, and sincerity. It has never been displeasing to us when opposing opinions are represented and spoken out amongst us. We believe that a free exchange of opinions can lead to the goal that a higher spirit, which does not originate from us, gives the final conviction.

The way to unity is never seen as dependent on the power of persuasion or argument.

> This unanimity can only come in a religious way, when God through his Spirit says the same thing to each individual as he says to the others. This unanimity does not take place through persuasion. (Quoted from an Eberhard Arnold mealtime talk at the Rhön bruderhof.)

Nevertheless, every bruderhofer knows that to find a united way is not easy. This helps them treasure even more the times when complete spiritual unity is given, when they find themselves fully united in things both great and small. Only then do the bruderhofers celebrate the Lord's Supper with one another which for them is one of the **highest** symbols of a believer's unity with God.

The ideal of unity also applies to marriage. The bruderhof teaches the indestructibility of marriage and true faithfulness. Accordingly, there are no divorces. People who become members of the bruderhof after a divorce are not allowed to marry again.

But unity is still more comprehensive. Eberhard Arnold said:

> Often it is like this; here is divine worship; here I serve God; and there is my profession in which I live for myself and my family. How can the unity and harmony with oneself and others be found in this way?

Christian discipleship applies to all areas of bruderhof life. There is no separation between work and free time, occupation and family, community and private life, "mine and thine." These are only different aspects of a united community together following Christ after the pattern of the early church.

At our first midday meal on the bruderhof, another

guest is present to share with the assembled circles of the three bruderhofs. Vincent Harding, a black church history professor from Denver, explains his work, his search for a radical Christian life and more community. He explains his research into the freeing of the slaves. He tells of the dire conditions which still existed 150 years ago in the United States and how the Christians took a leading part in both directions—by oppression of the slaves on the one side, and freeing them on the other side. It is a good arrangement and an interesting mealtime for us Europeans.

The bruderhofers are moved. The brother in charge asks the bruderhof men's choir to sing three Negro spirituals. Dozens of robust men in working clothes who have just come from the turning lathe in the factory stand up and go to the stage. Perhaps there are seventy of them, from young clean-shaven lads to gray-bearded pensioners. They begin to sing—and how they sing! The songs complement the address.

I am sitting opposite the stage and can see the men there. Many of them are barefoot as is common here in Woodcrest in the summer, with rolled-up trouser legs, dusty feet, or clumsy shoes. What a contrast—at ground level nothing but tough rustics, but above Vienna choirboys, beautifully singing, "We shall overcome."

Working, eating, singing—all in unity. Can mealtime be a consecrated feast of the community? Yes, today it really is—impressive and lovely, spontaneous and unexpected. At the several bruderhofs this mealtime will be the talk of the day, and they will discuss it during the midday break with their families and at the afternoon snack in their work areas. Community.

At two o'clock we are on the go again. I have difficulty

processing all the impressions. The experiences come too quick and fast.

On the way to the shop, as they modestly call the factory for Community Playthings, we see the bruderhof bus standing in the parking lot. The large yellow vehicle looks very American with its small nose in front. "Hutterian Brethren" is lettered clearly on its sides. It is their school bus.

In the bruderhof factory the work is done almost entirely by men. Our starting point is the metal shop, where the climbing frames, chassis, and accessories are made from aluminum. An aluminum welding plant is also located here. Numerous brothers are occupied welding, sawing, and filing. Just behind them is the paint room, where just now an endless belt of children's tricycles sprayed with yellow lacquer is hanging.

On the first floor of the building we find the assembly room. Here wheelchairs are assembled from the separate parts—quite complicated in their design for therapy of the handicapped. The bruderhof equipment items for the handicapped are all designed with advice from therapists. Five newly developed tricycles have just been sent to various therapy wards around the country for field-testing before beginning final production.

It is astonishing that here in the factory not only young and middle-aged people are working, but also the oldest brothers of the community—very friendly and dignified old men.

We have just learned to know Nils, an old brother from Sweden. He tells us that many years ago when he finished his engineering studies in Germany, he set off to wander through the German countryside. When he came upon the bruderhof in the Rhön, he didn't go any farther!

Passing through a storeroom of finished and packed goods, we reach the woodworking shop. Here the work is done entirely with maple, a beautiful, firm wood which is used by the truckload. A skilled brother, who with a quick glance can spot and make allowance for the knots and damaged places, cuts the maple boards to the exact length needed. These boards are then sawn lengthwise, planed, and passed through automatic molders. (Every other man we meet tells us that it is "from Germany." They all seem to think that we should feel at home in the presence of a German machine.) The machine spits out finished building bricks, wonderfully smoothed and beveled.

The ingenious brothers have constructed many machines for their specific purposes. A large community has a specialist who is particularly gifted for each task.

There are all kinds of other departments. In front of us tables are being screwed together. Here are stacks of sides for children's beds. Over there wooden trays are being lacquered—an unpleasant job because of the lacquer mist whirling around in the air.

But they take turns. Nobody is stuck permanently with the strenuous and difficult places of work.

Safety is stressed in this department. Each worker wears protective glasses and ear muffs to soften the noise. Over each machine hangs a special list of working instructions, together with safety measures which must be observed. The list details what in all events one must do, and what one must avoid! This is especially necessary because of the constant change of people operating on the machines. Some are high school boys who work as trainees there during the holidays or in the afternoons.

But not only safety instructions hang over the machines. Another notice attracted my attention all morning. Over the desks in the Community Playthings offices, over "big baby's" huge bulging eye in the laundry, over the changing table in the baby house—everywhere the most important rule of living together on the bruderhof is hanging. For over sixty years it has accompanied the bruderhofers and provided them with decisive direction for a community to function.

> "There is no law but that of love" (2 John 5:6). Love is joy in others. What then is anger at them? Passing on the joy that the presence of others brings us means words of love. Thus words of anger and worry about members of the brotherhood are out of the question. There must never be talk, either open or hidden, against a brother or a sister, against their individual characteristcs—under no circumstances behind their back. Talking in one's own family is no exception to this either.

> Without the commmandment of silence there is no faithfulness and thus no community. The only possible way is direct address as the spontaneous brotherly service to one whose weaknesses cause something in us to react negatively. The open word of direct address brings a deepening of friendship and is not resented. Only when one does not find the way together immediately in this direct manner is it necessary to talk together with a third person whom one can trust to lead to a solution and uniting in the highest and deepest. (Matt. 18:15-16)
> Each one in the household should hang this admonition up at his place of work where he always has it before his eyes.

So far as I can judge, they really expect this important rule to be followed—no gossiping about one another, no secrecy, no slander, no mockery.

Clearly, this ideal is not always achieved, but in general an atmosphere of trust and love is fostered in which feelings of inferiority or uncertainty can scarcely take root. This "first law" is not so much a stiff tradition as a daily necessity. One has to learn anew every day how to truly live in community.

The shop smells of work, of everyday normal life. It is fascinating that in this otherwise idyllic village such a professionally run workshop can be found. The desire to live in community all the time is obvious even in the factory. These are not the first timorous experiments in community which I have sometimes met in Germany. Here is a living organism with all that belongs to it—a foundry, a plastic molding press, a shipping department, and a full-color catalog. This community not only consists of nice people, exciting midday meals, and colorful folklore, but it represents a mastery of quite normal daily life, too.

It's time for the afternoon workshop tea break. We are just passing a worktable at which the black professor who spoke in the dining hall is laboriously smoothing the sharp edges of glued wooden boards with sandpaper. "There are no guests on the bruderhof, only co-workers," he tells us.

There is an idea, and ideal behind this rule. Perhaps the most important aspect of work on the bruderhof is commununity.

"We know that often in working together an inner contact can be given which endows work with a meaning," wrote Eberhard Arnold in May 1929. That still holds true today. On the bruderhof, community is celebrated! And work is included in this. Work should not determine the people; it should serve, not rule. The main thing is not through the incentive of wages to extract as much work as possible. One works for others, not for a boss. Work is a part of community with one another. There must be time for discussion. Fear and pressure must not rule. The work is quiet and concentrated, but not hectic.

That does not mean that the bruderhof is a haven for lazy, work-shy people, or that not much is produced. On the contrary, the six-day work week is still alive here. On Saturdays men are standing at their machines. But work, free time, communal life—these do not run in separate channels, but through and over one another. Community means serving one another, being there for one another, and that does not stop at the workshop door.

> The only reason for people's occupation is so often that with it they earn their bread and butter. For the rest, their life is unrelated to their profession. We fight against that. Just as there must be unanimity between people, so there must be unanimity between work and vocation. (From a report of a mealtime address by Eberhard Arnold during the time at Rhön)

Life, work, faith, community, all belong together in the eyes of the bruderhof. For this reason also, work does not begin at age sixteen and end at sixty-five. Because of this view of life and work, schoolchildren are sometimes drawn into the lighter tasks, and old folks join in the efforts as their strength allows. In this way they take part in the community life and are not left out.

There is no need for old folks' homes on the bruderhof. What for? They are in community; they are all there for one another. An eighty-year-old man spends hours daily in the archives transcribing old letters into English. An old sister stands an hour each day in the laundry ironing handkerchieves for the whole community, a service for all. In this lifestyle there is no loneliness in old age, no isolation, no little ghettos.

Today we are spared from this paradise of the workers and are allowed to relax. But tomorrow, punctually at eight o'clock I shall have to step in somewhere in the workshop.

For once, something different from an office desk, I think to myself, and I am full of anticipation.

6

A Symphony of Tools

Today we start to work—at eight o'clock. But actually here on the bruderhof a workout begins before work. This early morning workout is called "snacks"—breakfast, snack, and snack again.

Hermann carries with him a rather frightening list that gets longer and longer. It contains names of families who would like to invite us or whom we should definitely visit for our own interest. For this purpose, breakfast and those famous snacks are quite suitable. It seems as if snacks are the very heart of social life at the bruderhof.

Slightly exaggerated, here's how it goes. The alarm clock has just stopped its nervewracking ring. Hardly have I slipped into my trousers and buttoned up my shirt, when somebody very gently knocks on our door. As I open it, I see four little bruderhof children lined up before me, like organ pipes—each one cuter than the next. They are waiting to pick us up for breakfast. Because we don't know our way around yet, they come to show us.

"Just a moment," I say, as I hurry back into the room,

rub sleep out of my eyes, and take a comb and run it through my hair. Then a six-year-old boy takes my wife and me by the hand and decisively walks us down the steps and along the path toward the house just opposite, where a gigantic breakfast table is waiting for us. His seven brothers and sisters are eyeing us with great interest.

As usual, we are given the seats of honor at the table. A German song is selected of course. And for the third time— with twenty more to come—we sing, "Gutan Morgan, liebä Sonnä, an dem blauen Himmelszealt. Hast du aauch so gutt geschlafean wie wir hier auf dieser Wealt... ." ["Guten Morgen, liebe Sonne" with a strong American accent!].

Then we are allowed to take the first piece of bread, and start the meal. It's usually eggs and bacon, with toast. Here in America the bacon is always well done, so well done that only a little more work is needed to make it into tasty charcoal briquettes. And the toast which we get here is made of bread that even the Americans scoff at as airfilters. One can squeeze a whole loaf into a fistful of dough convenient for your luggage.

The coffee tastes mostly like air, but apparently that is the way processed coffee turns out here. One rare morning we had breakfast by ourselves, and someone painstakingly explained the process to us. It took us half an hour to learn it. One puts the coffeepot directly on the gas flame, pours water into the pot, and puts the coffee in some kind of a filter which is directly beneath the lid of the coffee pot. The lid has a little glass knob on top which enables us to watch the boiling water, heaving over and over seven times and slowly turning the appropriate brown. When the right color is achieved, the coffee is ready. Experts at Woodcrest have assured us that this procedure always works. The result of our own efforts was a fiasco.

If conversation lags, we have to think continually of something to tell that might be of interest. This is obviously more difficult because of our poor English. Sometimes I tear my hair in agony about the way I try to express myself—how much better I could say it in German!

Toward the end of our stay, after about fifty such experiences, we had developed a special vocabulary suitable for just those snacks and breakfasts.

Thirty-seven times we tell about the peace movement in Germany, 34 times about the acid rain, 31 times about the Green Party and their admittance to the Parliament. In addition we talk about Gollwitzer, Eppler, and Thielicke, and most certainly about the situation of the church in Germany, which no one here really understands.

We explain that liberal churchgoers are usually not so pious, and the pious are usually not so liberal, but that both usually attack the other with the same tactics which they have just condemned in the other. We mention that the Green Party is not so pious—but is for the peace movement, but not against abortion; that the pious are against abortion but do not belong to the Green Party and are not against the use of force, and so on and on. And if we don't tell all this on our own accord, then we are questioned. But we were warned already in the guest letter before we came here that there would be many questions. . . .

At the same time, we try to remember the different names and also do honor to the rather sweet sticky buns baked by the housewife. And, finally, squeezed out like a lemon and at the end of our strength, we leave that family five minutes before eight, because work is about to begin.

Perhaps I have exaggerated somewhat, but you can tell that we view the many snacks with mixed feelings. Yet, in spite of that, on such occasions we hear many interesting accounts and the wonderful life stories which led the different people to the bruderhof.

Again and again we are amazed how interested and sharing the people here are, and how eagerly they try to take part in things that happen. Excitedly they follow the growing peace movement in Europe. With real concern they listen to the reports of some of their guests about the countries they come from. They are alert and interested. It is this depth of human encounter, often with some of the older brothers and sisters, that provides the particular charm of the bruderhof. One does not sit with others in front of a TV, but one talks, lives, and has community.

Well now, after this early morning workout, the real day's work begins at eight. In the shop office, job assignments are handed out. Together with Timothy, a seventeen-year-old high school boy, we are led to a workbench stacked high with partly finished wood products. We are supposed to assemble them. Two men, two sides. What follows one might call, "A Symphony for Children's Beds with Compressed-Air Drills and Air Screwdrivers," played four-handed, of course.

After Nick, the foreman, introduces me to some of the skills and tools, we set to work. I feel like a high schooler just before the final exams. Timothy, who stands just opposite me and grins, has the know-how. He did it yesterday. A certain ambition grows in me. I want to demonstrate to myself that I can do more than just use a typewriter and a telephone. The whole job becomes a bit of a sport. Each time Timothy has to wait for me, a beginner, until I've finished my side of the crib. For understandable reasons, I want to avoid this, of course.

Every beginning is difficult, as the saying goes, but this air drill is actually pretty easy to work with. No problems. It goes into the wood like butter. Well now, we position the sides between the two end posts and put the hardware on it with four big screws which enter easily into the pre-drilled holes, and off we go, no problems. You see? I knew it! The screwdriver also works with air. It's a fantastic thing. It goes like the wind.

And now only four more little screws are needed. We put them right on the tip of the screwdriver, which is magnetic and holds the screw tight and in a vertical position. Very handy, I say to myself. Then I won't drill into my thumb when I hold the screw. So now, ready? I press the trigger and grrr, watch it!—where's the screw? Boy-oh-boy, try it again. It works for Timothy. Grrr! There you are. This time the screw does three turns before it flies against a wall somewhere. Bit by bit I learn how to put screws into the hard wood without pre-drilling.

And then, after some time, it begins to be fun. Timothy needs to wait less and less for me. Sometimes now I wait on him, if I put the screws here and the wheels over here and the other hardware on this place, he'd better look out! Things will go faster and maybe I can keep up. Maybe I will have to wait for him! After half an hour of this kind of training, I have mastered the routine sufficiently to be able to ask some questions and answer others.

To answer questions is always twice as strenuous because one first of all has to understand the question, while continuing to work at top speed. The younger the bruderhof members are, the faster they talk and the older I seem to be as I try to understand what they are trying to say.

We talk about high school, music, and Germany, and about the unbelievable speed limit in Germany—110, 120, even 130 miles per hour. This is mighty interesting for Timothy! He probably would love to try it once.

After two hours I've improved enough to keep up with the work and to enjoy it. In the meantime, the big piles of cribends have vanished just in time for a snack. Outside in front of the shop the men have arranged a few benches in a circle with a table in the middle. A nicely filled snack cart has been prepared by the kitchen staff. Everyone helps himself to some tea or juice or whatever he likes.

There are also a few oranges or apples again. The apples are eaten here with a thick layer of peanut butter.

One of the colleagues passes around a home-smoked catfish which he caught last week down by the river. Somewhere on the bruderhof there is a little smokehouse which anyone may use. We enjoy ample portions of the fish which, although caught in the mud of the river, tastes more fishy than muddy. And then we start an animated discussion about the churches in Germany. How is it with the peace movement there? What is the Green Party planning and what about the acid rain?

After our snack we resume making the cribs. By lunchtime we've managed to assemble enough of them to last for a few weeks.

The noon meal doesn't bring anything new. Slowly we begin to live normal lives again. But in the afternoon I find myself at a new workplace. At a special machine, I shape the armrests for chairs. Then, until the end of the day, I drill holes in some sort of tabletops.

By the end of the afternoon, surrounded by a symphony

of tools, I have actually managed to achieve a quiet, efficient work rhythm. Everyone has taken time to explain everything carefully to me. But it is good now to see and to hear something else again, because even here work isn't quite like paradise.

On the way to our room, I encounter Christel. She has spent most of the day at the preschool. Now I meet her with a whole group of children. They have learned some children's songs. Luckily, Christel could teach them a few German ones. Then they had a little party. What the reason was I do not know. To have celebrations, whether big or small, is a specialty of the bruderhofs.

Of course, Christel had to tell about the airplane trip to America. After she described in detail how wonderfully soft and foamy the clouds look from above, she was asked by a little boy whether one could open the windows of the airplane to stroke the clouds.

On a walk through the village, they admired a little bird's nest which they found near the "Sunnyside House." They noticed that one of the baby birds had fallen out of the nest. The whole group of children discussed excitedly what should be done about it. The bruderhof—with garden, shop, swimming pool, horse stables, and visitors— must seem to the little ones like one large playground full of adventure. How nice it would be to grow up in a place like this! Something is happening all the time. One is never alone. Things are always interesting, with endless surprises.

But on the bruderhof not only children may be happy. Everyone is free to experience enjoyment of all kinds. Joy, just for the fun of it, without a special reason, is not prohibited. The center of all the free-time summer activities is half a mile away—a small, specially dammed-up lake.

Here one can have a picnic, play, splash, or swim. The lake has separate sections for the children, the women, and the men, one big raft in the middle, and two lifeguards (one for the sisters, one for the brothers). But in an emergency, I was assured, that a lifeguard brother may pull out a drowning sister.

Also the winter has its joys. In January, if not earlier, Woodcrest has snow. Often, even better, the lake is frozen over. Then they go ice-skating and tobogganing. Whenever the bruderhofers do something, they go all out to do it right. The tobogganing track is several hundred yards long. It was carefully constructed. Its sweeping curves follow the contours of the rapidly falling slope, securely walled in with old car tires. The tobogganing track is an old tradition on the bruderhof. Already in Sannerz, the first bruderhof in the twenties, people enjoyed this winter fun. There the track was over two miles long. It started at the top of one of the highest hills, and swept nearly all the way down into the village. Daring, joyful games full of youthful enthusiasm appealed even to a doctor of philosophy!

But the people at Woodcrest don't like to keep such fun to themselves. They readily invite the neighbors or organize a festival for the children of the migrant workers of the Hudson Valley, whose parents often work under deplorable conditions in the fruit orchards. At harvesttime, the migrants move from one farm to the next, and often can buy only necessities at inflated prices in shops owned by the farmers. Sometimes they have entered the country illegally from places like Mexico or Central America and can be sent home at any moment. When the children of these migrant workers can experience a day of celebration in Woodcrest, things really get exciting, with barbecues, picnics, play, and games.

Last year the men temporarily removed sections of rollers used to transport the big cartons from the assembly area to the shipping end of the shop. With them they built a roller coaster on the hill, thrilling fun for the kids.

Is Woodcrest a holiday paradise? For the children of the bruderhof, that is almost a reality. The bruderhof is a sheltered children's land, consciously kept clean, a sane world shielded from the damaging influences of much of popular American society. They fear too much contact with the surrounding culture, especially for the children. Those who have met these pure and open and truly unspoiled children will understand. This is why it is basic for their life in community to have their own school. They try to protect the "childlike spirit" and the purity of their children. A spirit of expectation, of trust, and simple faith is something each member longs for in relationship to God. Great value is put on upholding a childlike spirit. They take seriously the warning of Jesus that anyone who misleads a little child in such a way that he cannot be a child anymore, it would be better for that person to be drowned in the sea.

In a certain way, the precious work with their children prevents them from being more deeply engaged with the world. I ask, "Wouldn't it be a good idea to live in the slums like other communities do and to work and live with socially deprived people?"

"Yes," they reply. "It would be a good thing—but our children. . . ."

They know how difficult it is to receive a Christian education under the influences of a worldly society. They observe other communities. For example, the Sojourners Community in Washington, D.C., has a good reputation at the bruderhof. But they are experiencing difficult problems in this very area, and are in dialogue with the members of the bruderhof. The bruderhof people see the mission among their own children as very important. No one becomes a member of the community automatically, not even their own children. They can't force them to live in the community. They are very careful not to pressure their children unduly to become adult members of the community, although it is one of the goals of their protective education. The joy is great of course when bruderhof children decide on their own accord to become members.

On the other hand, withdrawal and protectiveness do not mean overprotection. Seldom have I seen such wild and daring children as I met here. But to be daring is also a conscious goal in their education. The children are given free rein—whether to fall from a tree, be thrown from one of their horses, or jump into the water with their clothes on! It is better than to be a sissy. The children are present in everything and always active. There is no time for disco, or listening to the latest hits on a record player.

"We don't even have a TV, and use a radio only for the weather report," Hermann tells us.

This is not just a principle. One could find meaningful programs, he admits, but how could they find time for them in their very full schedule?

The bruderhof is well aware that, at least during high school age and the beginning of adolescence, every child goes through a process of becoming independent. Children should see how the outside world looks. They need to achieve a certain distance from the bruderhof to be able to consider and decide freely for life in community.

Obviously, all the teenagers are interested in how it is to attend Kingston High School, or later, a college somewhere. They feel a certain fear of new and strange places. At the local high school the group of the "Woodies" does not mix easily and holds itself apart from the other students. When school is over, they quickly vanish onto their seven hills.

Some time ago, the Woodcrest teenagers surprised their parents one day by closing ranks and deciding to identify more closely with the bruderhof. The girls agreed to wear their kerchiefs to school. The bruderhof had not required this out of consideration for them and as a protection against too much teasing by other students.

Perhaps the teenagers had also sensed a spirit in Woodcrest which does not need to hide itself, but has a lot to contribute. The boys joined in by wearing their bright blue bruderhof shirts to school, making them more obvious than before. But strangely enough, the more they are recognized, the more they are respected and the less they are laughed at.

"Since we've done that, we have had much more contact with our classmates," a fifteen-year-old told me. "At times they even come to us with their problems and ask us for advice." And there are enough problems for the Woodcrest teenagers to help find solutions to at Kingston High School. Nearly half of their classmates come from broken families. As many as 85 percent of American high schoolers reportedly have experimented with drugs. This is foreign to the experience of the Woodcrest young people, of course. Soon they realize what a privileged background they have. They like to help, offer an alternative, and challenge others through their lives. Their parents support this quite consciously. They also wish for more contact.

One step toward this was an official invitation from the bruderhof for the whole high school to a picnic on the Woodcrest grounds. Of about 2,500 students, approximately 150 accepted the invitation and experienced a nice day in the community, including a communal mealtime and later experiences in family groups.

The Woodcrest students are becoming more active in extracurricular activities at the high school. SAEV (Students Against the Extension of Violence) is one of the groups in which some of the Woodcrest high schoolers are active. Recently the high school principal encouraged more participation of bruderhof young people in school activities to help combat some of their problems.

Next weekend the high school choir is planning a trip to the Clearwater Festival. The young people have been asked to give a performance and tell something about the community. The folk singer Pete Seeger, an old friend of the community, invited them. He is the founder of the Clearwater Initiative, an organization for environmental protection of the polluted waters of the Hudson River. They will go and are eager for this new challenge. A year ago this would have been only a vague possibility.

We find that the communities are setting out on a new venture. They want to get out of their self-created isolation. They seek new contact. They are ready to reconsider old decisions. They enjoy the new stimulation that is brought to them by the growing number of guests. New life is coming into the bruderhofs.

7

Christian Utopia or Common Sense?

Guests, many guests, and also many new members—that was the situation in 1922, the first major crisis year for the barely 24-month-old community. Perhaps there were simply too many people and too many different views for the young community to deal with. Young people generally were beginning to feel division between themselves. The pastors of the different churches were calling young Christians back to the fold, arguing that the time of awakening was drawing to a close, and the people with "new eyes" should take their place in the old structures.

At Sannerz, Christian utopia and middle-class realism were locked in mortal combat. Could life in common really last? Could an individualistic modern person really give up self and be capable of community? Can one even today take the Bible and the witness of the early Christians quite literally? Such questions are just as pertinent today as then.

It appears that in community life, a succession of peaks and crises occurs—the closer the circle, the greater the struggles. The history of the bruderhof reflects this. The long simmering struggle in Sannerz finally came to a head over issues related to finance and faith.

In July 1922 a large loan to the Neuwerk Publishing House was suddenly recalled. Panic broke out: "What shall we live on? Wherever shall we find the money?" Eberhard and Emmy Arnold were in Holland just then with Kees and Betty Boeke, close friends who had often helped the young community financially. Betty Boeke, a relative of Cadbury, the chocolate king, offered occasional donations. She and her husband were themselves sympathetic with the idea of living without personal money or property.

The community at home wrote an urgent letter calling the Arnolds back at once. Something must be done. But Eberhard refused to return. He simply wrote that the money would be available on August 2, the date payment was due. This need must be met in faith, he said, and they should not expect his return before the deadline. Possibly Arnold had justifiable hope of raising the necessary money in Holland. Perhaps it was clear to him that in Germany, shaken by inflation and social crisis, there was no chance of raising the money. In any case, both he and Emmy saw that the payment of the debt was something which like all other problems in Sannerz must be handled out of the life of faith. Once again, the faith which expects the possible from the impossible stood against sound common sense.

On August 1, 1922, Arnold, singing peace songs, marched with Kees Boeke's circle and his family in a great peace march in Amsterdam. On August 2 the payment was due. In the evening an express train would bring them to Germany in time for the payment dealine in Frankfurt.

Shortly before their departure, a lady presented Arnold with an envelope of Dutch money, a present for the community. He exchanged the gulden for Reichmarks next morning at the bank in Frankfurt. The advantage of the stable gulden against the plummeting value of the Reichmark produced the exact amount of the debt to the last penny. When Arnold telegraphed the joyful surprise to the community, the answer came back: "Too late! The Neuwerk Publishing House is already liquidated." The "moneygroup" of the bruderhof had already given up.

Faith versus money; faith versus common sense! I can imagine that in that situation I might also have been in the money faction.

The Arnolds arrived home to an icy reception. To deal with the crisis, a meeting was called at once. It lasted late into the night and ended in a split. Forty members of the household wished to leave Sannerz and take the remaining stock of Neuwerk books with them. Seven remained— among them Eberhard and Emmy and Emmy's sister Else von Hollander. Fortunately, the house in Sannerz remained theirs, since the Arnolds had signed the contract. Seven people were left—the minimum number legally required to carry on the society. If one more had gone, everything would have had to be dissolved.

It took weeks until the "common-sense group" could leave the house completely. A depressing atmosphere of anti-community ruled the whole place. At last some of those forty found accommodation in another type of community, the Habertshof in Schlüchtern.

Once more the Arnolds and the few faithful ones stood before a void—yet with confident faith and hope. New guests came who had heard about the sensational dissension in the community and wanted more exact information. Again the bruderhof began to grow.

The years of rebuilding were characterized by spontaneity, joy, great enthusiasm, and an ever stronger sense of community. Families joined and orphan children were taken in. Already by 1926 it was necessary to look intensively for a new place with larger accommodations. They soon located "Sparhof," a farmstead of seven separate buildings in a very poor and isolated part of the Rhön. This would be the home for the bruderhof for the next eleven years. In November 1926 a first group moved in and began to improve the facilities. In 1927 the rest of the community and the Eberhard Arnold publishing house followed.

The spiritual attitude and inner life of the Arnolds and the community had been strongly influenced by religious socialists. These had included the Swiss Hermann Kutter, and especially the *Wurttembergischen* pietist father and son Blumhardt. But now in 1928 in addition to those, the bruderhofers for the first time came to a decisive encounter with the Hutterians. Eberhard Arnold himself later described his inner development as moving from "Lutter [Luther] to Kutter to Hutter."

The community began in that year to go deeply into the Anabaptist history of the sixteenth century, and was especially moved by the example of the early Hutterians. In the life and thought of these martyrs they discovered kindred spirits to themselves. When they heard that Hutterians still existed in the United States and Canada, they decided to make contact. Perhaps they should join these Hutterians since they had no interest in simply building up a new movement of their own. A letter was sent off with the request to become part of them.

The economic straits of the bruderhof in 1928 may have contributed to this decision. It is true that there was growth, living community, and enough work; but the fi-

nancial situation was more than depressing. They had
hardly started at the Rhön when they were threatened with
being auctioned. The auctioneer turned up quite regularly
to identify the items he would offer for sale. Frequently
brothers were sent out to raise money from friends and
supporters to prolong credit terms and satisfy the creditors.
On one occasion the enforced auction was stopped only at
the last moment.

They eagerly awaited the answer from the Hutterians
abroad. After a long time, a short letter came with a few
booklets, and bit by bit a correspondence developed. It
soon became clear that in matters of faith this was the right
direction to turn. The Hutterians were still living together
after four hundred years in authentic Christian community
of goods and complete pacifism, practiced adult believer's
baptism as the bruderhof did, and had besides a rich
treasury of experience to share on how a community could
best be organized and built up. But a trip to America was
needed to establish closer contact.

Before the journey began in spring 1930 (it lasted more
than a year), Eberhard Arnold made an extensive study of
the sources and edited a history of the Anabaptists of Wurt-
temburg. He worked himself so deeply into the Hutterite
history that his knowledge of it aroused respect and much
admiration among the Hutterian brothers when he traveled around the colonies on his own. This extremely difficult mission which demanded his whole strength was also
a deep and joyful experience. An extensive diary of his
journey witnesses to this. The trip was made more difficult
from the beginning by a serious eye inflammation. Nevertheless, Arnold managed in the course of the next twelve
months to visit all 33 Hutterite bruderhofs, speaking with

the elders, and little by little winning the trust of the brothers.

The impressions which he gathered in the Hutterian colonies were quite varied. Almost always he was met with great love and sympathy. As a special honor he was frequently given the bedroom of the elder. Once he even shared the elder's double bed. Naturally, the Hutterian brothers wanted to hear everything about the new community in Germany and he had to tell of it for hours on end. He was asked many detailed questions, including, "Is your wife also nice and plump?"

"Here that is seen as the one and only ideal of womanly beauty," Arnold wrote to his wife. "Then when I show your picture, Emmy, although actually I try to avoid this, they call out, 'Oh, look, to be sure Emma, is beautiful!' and they admire me twice as much."

There was not only warm sympathy, but also frosty reserve. Many colonies still breathed the early Hutterian spirit, while others appeared rigid and far away from the true Hutterianism. Arnold was especially disturbed by the division of the Hutterites into three distinct groups: Lehrer, Schmiede, and Darius people (which, by the way, remains essentially the same today). That wealthy colonies existed side by side with colonies heavily in debt, seemed to him not in keeping with the spirit of the early Christians. Familiar with the sources and witnesses of the Hutterian forefathers, Arnold spoke to them openly and sharply about these impressions. Through this, fruitful talks and exchanges valuable for both sides took place.

For Arnold, another contradiction seemed to be their acceptance of technical progress and employment of machines in their work, while still holding to strict outward forms in many other areas. The Hutterian clothing goes back to the old Tirolean peasant costume. Images (pictures) and musical instruments are completely rejected as "Catholic." And while the smoking habit of some of the Arnold bruderhof people brought objection, yet the Hutterites had no conscience against their own use of alcohol.

Arnold kept members of the bruderhof in Germany informed regularly by letters. Some of the new orders and rules which they heard came to them as a shock. They did not wish to submit to new laws which had not come out of their own experience and which had no meaning for them. Hot discussions flared up. Finally Eberhard's spiritual insight settled the matter. He declared that they also belonged to the communal Christian movement which arose in Reformation times, and that the decision to join the Hutterites stemmed in part from their financial need and the isolation they felt from Christians in Germany.

In December 1930 the uniting with all three Hutterian groups took place. By the laying on of hands Eberhard Arnold was appointed as a "servant of the Word" and as elder for Germany, with all the rights and duties of an elder, an event without any precedent or parallel in Hutterian history.

However, the strong hope for financial support from the brothers was not fulfilled, in spite of another five months of visiting and repeated intense requests. (As Arnold wrote in a letter dated December 1930, "There is only one way to move these fortresses, that is a continuous siege.") When Arnold arrived at last in Bremerhaven in May 1931, he left the ship *Berlin* with only a trifling sum in his hands.

Nevertheless, uniting with the Hutterians was an enrichment—and not only for the community in the Rhön. The old Hutterians told of an awakening through Arnold's admonishing sermons, and through his "fire of the first love." Arnold himself said in a speech taken down in short-hand, shortly after his return on May 15, 1931, concerning the uniting with the Hutterians: "I am of the opinion that our turning to Hutterdom means that we become early Hutterian. We do not want to become Hutterian in the sense of 1930, but we want to become Hutterian in the sense of 1529-1589, in the sense of those first sixty years. With this the Hutterians are in agreement: the spirit of early Sannerz, the early Christians, the early Hutterians, of early mankind. . . ."

But submitting to the lesser rules of the Hutterians was not easy for the bruderhofers, so strongly influenced by the German youth movement. It was relatively easy to combine the Hutterian costume with that of the youth movement and similar styles, but the renunciation of their simple and beautiful pictures, flutes, and guitars, was far more difficult.

In the years before 1933 the danger lay merely in inner tensions and great material need. But Hitler's coming to power in January 1933 brought a threat from outside, and suffering for the bruderhof. This history of persecution, banishment, and exile would easily fill an unusual and highly gripping book.

Soon on the Sparhof (the community in the Rhön), they became aware that the National Socialist movement would give them the bad name of primitive Christian communists. Eberhard Arnold, in close contact with the authorities in Fulda and Kassel, tried again and again to explain the position of the bruderhof members: "We cannot go along with the policy of 'coming in line' nor com-

bine the following of Christ with National Socialism—they
cannot coincide. We cannot greet anyone with 'Heil
Hitler' (salvation by Hitler) because salvation comes from
God alone!"

In spite of the threatening situation, 21 new members
were baptized on Easter 1933. The community wanted to
to still be a witness. Again and again Eberhard Arnold
concerned himself with the possibility of coming persecution, and tried to prepare the community. In the summer
of 1933, a large number of novices left the bruderhof out of
fear. On the way home from a visit to the district leader of
the Nazi Party, Eberhard broke a leg. The complicated
break was treated for several weeks in the hospital, but it
never really healed.

In November 1933 a national plebiscite was held in
which Hitler's policies were expected to be openly confirmed. The authorities made clear to the members of the
bruderhof that their presence and agreement at the voting
places was expected. United in their rejection of Hitler,
they did not want to answer simply with a "no." So
Eberhard prepared a declaration which each one copied
onto gummed paper, and on the day of the vote in
Veitsteinbach stuck to the ballot. The declaration made
clear that they wished to obey the government but could
not support Hitler's actions. To the astonishment of the
bruderhofers in the next day's newspaper the result of the
referendum appeared as "100% Yes."

However, on November 16 the reaction to the coura-
geous opposition of the bruderhofers took place. In the first
light of dawn the Sparhof was surrounded and thoroughly
searched by 160 SS, SA, and Gestapo men. The official
charge pointed to a "suspicion of the formation of a com-

munist group." Eberhard Arnold was accused by false witnesses of having called for a violent revolt. Only the fact that he lay in bed recuperating from leg surgery saved him from the concentration camp. After searching the bruderhof thoroughly and finding no weapons, the Nazis left with stacks of papers and books. "Especially books bound in red," the bruderhofers recall with a smile, "because they wanted to prove that we were communists."

A few days later the school superintendent of the Fulda district stood before the door of the little bruderhof school to find out whether the bruderhof children were "nationally minded." He was there to observe whether they used the "Heil Hitler" greeting, for example, and knew the Horst-Wessel song. Naturally, the test turned out badly and the school was closed. After Christmas a Nazi teacher was to take over the instruction. The bruderhofers acted quickly. When at the beginning of January the Nazi teacher appeared, all the children were gone. They had found refuge with friends in Switzerland.

From this time on, the pressure of the National Socialist authorities on the community got worse. The bruderhof was forbidden to take overnight guests. By this ploy their hospitality toward visitors was greatly hindered. Only by "tricks" were they able now and again to put up guests. The next measure was an order forbidding the sale of books of their publishing house and of wooden crafts. This was the community's only source of income. Suddenly a loan to the bruderhof was recalled and had to be paid back. The Nazis made life in the Rhön more and more difficult for the 120 people of the community. There was often literally no money in the house, and the food was worse than scanty. It soon became clear that alternative quarters must be found, especially for the young people in danger of being called up for military service.

In March 1934 a possible location in Liechtenstein was found—an empty summer hotel at 4,000 feet elevation in the mountain highlands. And so the Alm bruderhof at "Silum" began. In March 1935 the first seventeen young men had to leave the Rhön in the dead of night. They headed separately toward Liechtenstein by various means of transportation.

That spring Eberhard's nephew, Hermann Arnold (our faithful friend and guardian today) came to the bruderhof. His conversion to Christ and the attitude of the Nazis toward the Jews had convinced him that he could not in good conscience remain in the SA which he had joined in his youthful enthusiasm. So he sent his uniform back (an action which could easily have doomed him to the concentration camp) and joined the group of young men on the Alm bruderhof.

But the situation in Liechtenstein was not easy either. The National Socialist party of Liechtenstein worked against the bruderhofers and gathered material and signatures to force the government of Liechtenstein to expel the community. At once Eberhard Arnold traveled to the Alm bruderhof and spoke with the government. The officials told him to appeal directly to the people, because the government would not be able to protect the bruderhof.

So a public meeting was arranged and Eberhard spoke to a crowd in front of the entrance of a church. Some Nazis began to whistle and throw stones. Eberhard called out, "If you want to oppose what I here witness to God, then come up and tell me to my face!" The disturbances stopped and the atmosphere in Liechtenstein improved.

In 1934 and 1935 Eberhard and Emmy had not only outside pressures to deal with, but difficulties also appeared in the inner life of the two separated bruderhofs. The Arnolds traveled again and again to the Alm to advise and assist in the recurring outbreak of conflicts there. In spite of these efforts, a strong moralistic/legalistic spirit took more and more control. Also some of the leading brothers struggled to gain power over one another.

Hardly had this crisis been overcome, when a similar conflict broke out in the Rhön. Cliques, gossiping, and narrow-mindedness developed on the one hand, and toleration of evil on the other. Eventually the Rhön bruderhof was no longer a living community organism and hardly had any life left in it. In a last desperate step it took on church discipline and placed itself under the inner leading of the Alm bruderhof, which sent some of the older experienced members back to the Rhön. The hope was that with new love for God and the brothers and sisters, repentance and turning around would take place.

On November 22, 1935, in the midst of this turmoil, the young Hutterian community reeled under the heaviest blow yet. Eberhard Arnold, their founder and elder, died unexpectedly.

A second operation on the unhealed leg had become necessary. Complications occurred and the leg had to be amputated by emergency surgery, but even this step came too late. Now the life-bearing center, the spiritual-leading personality of the community, the man of vision, had left them. There was no one else who could lead them back again and again to the biblical witness. No one else who could settle a difficult situation with a clear word. Agony struck the community. How could they go on? Who would lead them and keep them together in this and in every distressing situation?

But the affiliation with the Hutterians and their firm community structures now bore its fruit. Eberhard Arnold—although without any concrete premonition—had made provision that the community should withstand his death. Even though in coming years it was those very Hutterian rules and prohibitions which provoked discord among their leaders, yet belonging to the larger community at this point held them together. Of course the threat from outside also bound them together and required immediate action. Both factors together helped the community to survive the next years.

Crisis after crisis followed. Some were covered over and, through the demands of outer pressures, hardly noticed; others were quite open and painful. Eberhard Arnold's death wounded the community more deeply than they realized. In some respects the bruderhofs have actually only quite recently recovered from his death. The shockwaves of this experience were alive in the community until the 1970s. The planned move to the Alm bruderhof proceeded, but the guiding witness of Eberhard Arnold became more and more watered down or covered over by other focus points and directions.

In spring of 1936, the situation even in Liechtenstein became too dangerous. Hitler was pressing the Liechtenstein government to expel all Germans of military age. It was not possible for this tiny country to protect the bruderhofers any longer.

Arnold and Gladys Mason, a young English couple, through meeting Eberhard's son Hardy in England (where he was studying because of Nazi pressures) had been moved to join the bruderhof. The Masons had previously been sent back to England and were now asked to look for a suitable place for a new bruderhof.

Meanwhile the young men all left the Alm bruderhof to try to reach England by roundabout ways. Some managed by way of Italy and France to get through to England. These were adventurous journeys, often without money, or visas, or necessary papers. Frontiers were crossed at night. One young man, when almost to safety, was denied admittance to England by the immigration authorities. But little by little they each succeeded in getting to England. In March 1936 a new bruderhof was founded—the Cotswold bruderhof near Ashton Keynes in Wiltshire.

In summer 1936, while Adolf Hitler was honored in Berlin during the Olympics, the struggle against the bruderhofers continued. With hardly any money, almost nothing to eat, and dependent upon the support of faithful friends, Emmy Arnold and one of the brothers traveled to Amsterdam to the Mennonite World Conference. There they made important friends who would later help in many ways. But they were also indignant at how much the German Mennonites went along with the spirit of the times, and betrayed the actual Anabaptist attitudes regarding war and the state.

April 14, 1937, was the end of the bruderhof in Germany. On the grounds of the famous "order for the protection of the people and the state from communistic power tactics," the last remaining bruderhofers in the Rhön received orders to leave Germany on a day's notice as "unwanted persons." Their premises were confiscated. Fortunately, two Hutterian brothers from America visiting the Rhön as foreigners could not be interfered with by the

Nazis. Because of their presence perhaps some harsher actions were not carried out. Nevertheless, three brothers, because of the "anger of the people," were taken into "protective custody" by the Gestapo and later accused of "criminally falsifying the accounts." Two mornings later the rest of the community left the now empty building in a sad procession. They could take with them only what they could carry. Six adults and one child got through to the Alm bruderhof. Eighteen adults and thirteen children were brought under police escort to the Dutch border, and on the other side were lovingly taken in by Mennonites.

After three months, the three imprisoned brothers were set free by a friendly judge during the absence of the Gestapo leader from Fulda. Evidence of the suspicion against them was not found, and the proceedings were postponed. By daring means the three arrived near the Dutch border. At night, armed with map and compass, they made their way through the German forest to Holland, then lost their way and stumbled onto German territory again. On a second attempt they were discovered by border guards, who miraculously allowed them to cross the border again. The guards even showed them the road to Holland. A little later they arrived safely at the English bruderhof.

Following the annexation of Austria by Germany on March 13, 1938, the last community members of the Alm bruderhof had to leave Liechtenstein.

But the group grew. More and more contacts with young English people occurred, some of whom joined the community. Soon the Cotswold bruderhof grew too small, offering too little accommodation and too few possibilities for work. A second community was established—"Oaksey

Manor," an old manor house with a farm attached, five miles from the Cotswold bruderhof. The intended real-estate transaction led to a mistrustful question in Parliament. "Did the English government know that the Oaksey property was to be sold with the intention of accommodating 300 German families? Moreover this property is surrounded by five airfields, some of which have strategic importance . . . ."

But the Home Office saw no reason for stopping the sale. Nevertheless, among the local population opposition to selling to "the Germans" continued. Petitions were signed and the bruderhof found it necessary to hold open meetings to explain their Christian convictions and way of life. On March 26, 1939, the Oaksey bruderhof was founded. Later the Tellings Farm was also secured. The growing community needed accommodation and the means for earning an income.

Meanwhile on September 1, 1939, Germany brought on the Second World War by her conquest of Poland. On September 3, England reacted by declaring war on Germany. The situation of the bruderhofs now became much more complicated. In May 1940, the German campaign against Holland, Belgium, and France began. The English army was trapped at Dunkirk and escaped only with much difficulty.

The fear of invasion grew in England along with the mistrust of the "German" bruderhofs. The sale of bread, milk, and eggs, which provided the main part of the bruderhof income, was hindered by boycott and had to be given up. The German members were subject to a curfew after eight o'clock in the evening and were threatened by the local inhabitants. Wild rumors circulated. Some reported seeing "bruderhof people sending signals into the sky with flashlights." The fields around the bruderhof were bordered with concrete blocks to prevent German aircraft from landing. A young Englishwoman, eight days after her marriage to a German member, was confined for six weeks in an English concentration camp on the Isle of Man because by marriage she had automatically become an "enemy alien."

When the bombing of England began, the situation became even worse. In the summer of 1940 the community decided to ask the Home Office for permission to leave England as a whole—the last possible way to remain together, as the German members were in acute danger of being interned in English concentration camps. The Home Office was friendly and cooperative. They allowed the emigration, even arranging for ship passage and cabin accommodations.

A feverish search began for countries willing to accept the community. All attempts failed. Even the United States and Canada were not willing to receive them in spite of the efforts made by the Hutterian Brethren. As it turned out, the only country which would let the bruderhof in was Paraguay. So the women sewed mosquito nets and gathered information on how to prepare themselves for a subtropical country in South America. But there was little information available and their impressions of the strange country remained vague. What awaited them in faraway Paraguay, the bruderhof could not have imagined in its most fearful visions.

In December 1940 the first group left Liverpool on a steamer of the Blue Star Line. They traveled first class because no other accommodations were available. Although this was a severe drain on the community treasury, they could sun themselves for some weeks in the luxury of the *Andalucia Star* with their own waiters and princely food. The pleasantries of the trip were a deceptive and extremely fragile calm before the storm which awaited them in the hot wastelands of the Paraguayan Chaco. It was quite deceptive, for at any moment the ship could be struck by a German torpedo as they traveled through the U-boat blockade of England. In continual fear and making wide zigzags outside the usual mapped-out routes, ship and passengers reached Buenos Aires on December 21.

On Christmas Day they landed at Asuncion, the capital of Paraguay, aboard a stinking dirty river steamer, their first stopover on the way to the not yet existing bruderhof.

It had taken the old ship three days to steam up the Parana River with eighty bruderhofers and all their worldly goods. For three more days they waited in the sweltering summer heat of Asuncion on the steamer which was to take them to Puerto Casado. From there they went by train to "Kilometer 145," where friendly Mennonites with horses and wagons met them. The Mennonites took them another hundred kilometers to Colony Fernheim, where the bruderhofers spent the next three months waiting.

Meanwhile the brothers fanned out to find a suitable place to settle. At last they discovered and purchased an estate called "Estancia Primavera." It was a large property of over 20,000 acres in the wilderness, forty miles from the river, the nearest link to civilization. So the entire community began the journey by truck, river steamer, and ox wagons. In Primavera there was only one house and no hygienic conveniences. A group of men went ahead and began to build primitive houses with roofs of palm leaves and without walls. Soon women and children followed. Everyone suffered from mosquito, heat, insects, and the unbelievably primitive conditions.

Next a sawmill was built. Soon a new group arrived from England. Wells were dug and a steam engine set up. Nearly all the community suffered severe infections. The children were especially hard hit. During 1941 the balance of the group arrived from England, except for three members who remained to wind up the sale of the properties there.

More than 350 bruderhof people had come safely to Paraguay in more than ten different ships. There were storms—but nothing serious happened. On one of the voyages, a child was born. On the return trip or on later journeys all the ships which had brought the community members to South America were without exception torpedoed and sunk.

The last groups to arrive found the brothers and sisters in great need. They were all still living in the primitive houses without protection from the night cold, exposed to rain and the weather. There was little food and much sickness. In the first three years, twelve children died. Added to this, soon after the arrival of the first group in Paraguay, struggles concerning direction and leadership broke out again. The three sons of Eberhard Arnold, now grown to maturity, wanted to continue to lead the community in the spirit of their father. But they were rejected and sent away from the community for a time. Again inner need was added to the outer need. Only slowly was it possible to establish the life of the *Sociedad Fraternal Hutteriana*, the Hutterian Society of Brothers.

The three members who stayed in England experienced

something quite different. New friends, mostly pacifists, joined the no longer existing bruderhof. By Christmas 1941 there were nineteen such persons. In February 1942 it was decided in Paraguay to build up a new bruderhof in England, since any new members there were ineligible for emigration. In March 1942 the work began at the new Wheathill bruderhof. It soon became clear that the little community needed help. All the members with experience in agriculture were in Paraguay. So it was decided to send three couples back to England. By 1952 the Wheathill bruderhof had grown to over 200 members.

Already in 1942 the main community in Paraguay established a second bruderhof on their large piece of land. The *estancia* in Primavera now consisted of the Isla Margarita and the Loma Hoby communities. Besides these, a house in Asuncion was rented for selling bruderhof products and as a place where the young people could live who were in training in the capital. In 1946 a new community in Ibate followed, actually planned as a home for 130 orphan children from Germany, now destroyed by war. A number of journeys to the home country were undertaken, but the plans fell through. Instead, 110 displaced persons arrived from German camps in 1948. But gradually they left. Only one of them ever joined the community.

By 1950, through births and newcomers, the number of members of the bruderhof in Paraguay had grown to over 600. Apparently the community had stabilized itself, found its way back to unity, and the question of leadership was clarified. But the economic basis remained weak, barely sufficient for the most essential needs. The community lived in real poverty. Some money had been found through lecturing and fund-raising journeys to the United States—

particularly for newly established hospital work. They had contact especially with Quakers. In 1948 for the first time interested people visited the community from the United States and important new connections were established.

In October 1950 a visit with serious consequences took place. Two Servants of the Word of the Hutterian colonies in Canada visited Primavera. It became clear that the "old" and "new" Hutterians had grown apart. The brothers were welcomed at Primavera in a friendly way, but they were shocked by what they saw. Especially the outward lifestyle caused tension. The youth movement background of the bruderhofers had again intruded strongly. Many Hutterian rules had been annulled to make things more "attractive" for new members. Music, folk dancing, and especially smoking were offensive to the brothers. The appropriate warning of the two Servants of the Word was proudly rejected. After the two Hutterians returned to Canada, another warning and challenge to repentance was given but ignored. The unity with the Hutterian brothers which had lasted twenty years was approaching the breaking point.

What had been built up under Eberhard Arnold to hold the community together and to be a corrective element was now eliminated. False directions came in. Also in England on the Wheathill bruderhof the seeds of new problems had long been growing. Faith in human reason and in one's own strength had once more become stronger than unity in the Spirit and trust in God's power and leading. So in 1957 the bruderhof at the height of outward strength—with 1,400 people from twenty nations at ten locations in five different countries—was on the brink of its most serious downfall.

8

Increasing by Decreasing

There are times when life in the bruderhof is like a yo-yo. One minute you're up, the next you're down. Calms and crises follow each other in rapid succession. It's no different for visitors. Initially you're hit with the bright colors, the uniqueness, the unexpected. Wow! Who would have thought that such a life exists!

After a few days all this fades and reality emerges. No, the people are not, after all, haloed saints wafting from place to place. They're normal human beings—some pretty, some plain; some loud, some quiet; some thinkers, some doers—in short, quite normal people with normal faults, weaknesses, and problems. Upon observing this, you begin to calm down.

Next you notice that what seemed to be a little paradise on earth is not exactly that. There's hard work here—not only at the ripsaw or in the offices, but on yourself, and on the community. It is often painful and sobering work.

And still later you begin to see that what was at first fascinating, unique, and compelling has become strenuous, trying, and even irritating. Then you remember the time-worn adage, that there is no such thing as a free lunch. Nothing is going to fall into your lap here anymore than it would somewhere else.

At this point that you begin to wonder, Can I live like this? Do you *want* to live like this? And a little critical elf starts to whisper into your ear (especially if you've just gotten up after a sleepless night, or just walked away from a conversation you wish you'd never had), "Where have all the flowers gone?" Pink glow—schmink glow? Get me out of here!

I am pretty sure this experience is not confined to guests. No one can be perpetually jolly. People's feelings fluctuate. Their attitudes waver. I myself am wavering. There's a lot I'd have to give up to live like this and I'm not sure it's worth it.

How in the world can anyone live like this? It doesn't take long to receive an answer to this at the bruderhof. But it takes time to go beyond hearing the answers and to get to the point where you are absorbing them and feeling what they mean. "If you come to the bruderhof, wanting to live here, you must be ready to surrender yourself completely. This means your wishes, your plans, and your ideas have to die. It means surrendering yourself every day." How often I heard that.

Of course, those who want to follow Christ and live as the early Christians did must let their selfish desires die, giving themselves up for the sake of Christ and service to others. But there is a wide gulf between accepting these answers in theory and actually practicing them. It helps to have the life here before your eyes, though. The idealistic dream of community evaporates fairly soon.

Although the members do not speak of it often, they know that such surrender is certainly not possible in your own human strength. Anyone who tries it soon gets to the end of his tether. All have had dramatic experiences of this. To give yourself up, to make a lifelong commitment, assumes a complete turn toward Christ as the source of strength. Only through Christ can one live in love, community, and humility. "Finding yourself," for them, means finding Christ and following his example. "Realizing Christ" means making faith, trust, and discipleship real in your daily life.

The bruderhof demand of self-surrender is not a call to severe asceticism, personal suppression, and a restricted lifestyle as is the case with these who try to surrender themselves in their own strength. To die to yourself, to be a servant of Christ, a servant of the community actually involves finding yourself by giving yourself up. This sounds absurd in human terms. The people of the bruderhof, however, have experienced that it is not nonsense. It is a concept that works, while at the same time remaining a deep mystery. Only if a seed falls into the ground and dies, will it bear fruit. That's how Jesus Christ expressed it as recorded in the New Testament.

That is the ideal of life in the bruderhof. To make a creative sacrifice, to grow through diminishing, to achieve more through less—this apparent contradiction can be experienced in this community. Paradoxically, the personality grows, becomes richer, more rounded, more perfect, if the ego dies. I observe here that self-surrender does not produce gray, ascetic, sad monks, but happy and normal people, who have apparently found their calling and their identity.

But even if you grasp this spiritual mystery, you do not find it easy to live it. To live in community for sixty years means more than being enthusiastic or convinced. It takes one's total continuous commitment to live in such a radical way.

"One who comes here has usually tried everything else," I am told. For many people the bruderhof is the last chance to live in community. "We choose this way only if we have suffered shipwreck with all other things," they tell me. To be a decisive Christian is described in a similar way in the New Testament. To be a Christian, contrary to what some pious people want to make you believe, is no sluggish hobby for quiet evening hours. It is not a little of eternity's incense for a quiet middle-class life, not a moral code of behavior.

To be a Christian means turning around your whole life, everything, a change of your entire nature. Many people in the bruderhof can tell you how long it took them till they grasped that their whole life needed to change at the core of their being. Social duties, communal life, or ethical norms are the results (not the essence) of a changed life. To live as the early Christians did requires a complete turning around, and perceiving all of life in a new way.

Certain kinds of careers have sometimes led to the bruderhof. Persons may have been active in social movements, in peace groups, in food cooperatives, and trade unions. After a time of struggle they began to see that the aims of these groups were too narrow, too sectarian. To change society they needed to work for change in a broader way. Consequently, they joined a radical community movement or founded one themselves. But these attempts did not lead to the goal either. Again and again the attempts to live in community were shipwrecked—in most cases because of the egos of the individual members.

Then perhaps they went to another community. Here too they soon experienced crises and breakdown, until they heard of the bruderhof which emphasizes social as well as communal responsibility on a spiritual foundation able to bear the load. The bruderhof had experienced some decades of more or less successful communal history without falling apart. For many, the bruderhof represented the last attempt for an alternative life—and in most cases it worked out all right.

But it is not easy to be accepted in the community of the bruderhof. "Usually it is quite easy to become a member of a youth cult, but it is very hard to get out of it. With us it is the other way around," says one of the members. "To become a full member with us is not easy, but it is easy to leave the community again."

I can—at least—confirm the first part of the statement. Normally the path to the bruderhof starts with a short informative visit. For many it ends there. Quite quickly you see whether you can imagine living such a life at all. If there is further serious interest, a second and often a third visit is arranged. Between these visits are long intervals for thinking and examining one's motives. Only then can you ask the community for acceptance into the novitiate. This is granted if the community is absolutely sure that the applicants are serious and know what they are facing. Still, during the past year nine novices from outside have found their way to the bruderhof. After a time, the decision of novitiates is confirmed through baptism.

To become a novice means to place oneself under the guidance and correction of the community and to promise to be faithful unto death—a vow that has become bitter reality for many Old Hutterians. When new members begin their novitiate they transfer all their property to the community, giving up all rights to it. They agree to live in full community of goods with the other members. They acknowledge that they will have no right to have their property restored in case they ever would leave the brotherhood again.

This rule—necessary for the community—makes the way back to the old life not as easy as it sounded in the above quoted sentences. For which family with several children finds it easy to face an uncertain future? Which person wants to wonder if sufficient resources will be available to sustain themselves in old age or in extended illness?

Only on carefully considered grounds would persons break off their chosen decision and lose everything. Of course, the community is not a heartless group that would leave their ex-members in poverty. Help is given as far as is feasible. But this decision is in the hands of the community—there is no legal right. That is a weighty reason for not taking the entering into membership lightly. The community wants to be sure that one does not join out of romantic idealism. The clear call and commitment to life in community, and the costs of this decision, must be clear.

Of course, for the children of the bruderhof, it is easier. They come back to what they have known, while others need to give up their previous way of life. The community carefully examines their own novices to determine that their desire to become members is spiritually motivated and not simply a desire to continue a way of life they have enjoyed together.

Community of goods is probably the hardest require-
ment for people from outside who are seriously interested
in a life like this. Money means freedom, freedom to go
somewhere in your car, to enjoy a vacation, to buy something for yourself. Outside the bruderhof the measure of
freedom often depends on the amount of cash in one's
purse or in a bank account. Here people do not have
money in their pockets. The children sometimes do not
even know what those round little metal buttons are which
play such an important role in the outside world. You do
not need money in the bruderhof. Each person gets what is
needed from the steward or housemothers. These few
people in the community have to deal with money in a
practical way. They do the purchasing, look after the bank
account, pay the bills, and have financial oversight.

If you need new shoes, trousers, or shampoo, you ask the
housemothers. They are careful that no injustice occurs,
that one person does not receive more than the others. Nobody is entirely free from possessiveness even in the midst
of the most radical community of goods. Though the need
for personal possessions diminishes, the inner struggle
against egoism and striving for property remains.

The care of personal property is not a matter of indif-
ference to the bruderhof. What you have, you have
received from the community, therefore you are responsible for it to the community. It is not unusual for one to
apologize for leaving the gas burning overnight or losing
their shoes in the woods. Community means surrendering
to one another—responsibility for one another. Therefore
one does not demand or insist on alleged rights. "The other
has such and such. Why can't I?" On the contrary. A
weekend excursion for the young people, for example, is a

gift from the bruderhof, not something that is considered as a right.

The tasks of the housemothers and the steward are not always easy. Often difficult decisions have to be made. What is good and what goes beyond the mark? What fits the goal of living simply and in a responsible way and what is irresponsible extravagance? Again and again the community corrects itself in such matters. Sometimes it is established that the food has become too good, so expenditure on foodstuffs is cut down. Or one notices that after hard years there is the danger to act according to the resources presently available. "Now we can afford it—there is enough money!"

"Again and again we have to examine if our usage of money is done in a responsible way," the young steward from Woodcrest tells us.

"For instance, Sunday trips in a car have been reduced pretty much. It just became too much a matter of fact to ask for a car to go to the Catskill Mountains. We noticed this and decided in the community to live less luxuriously in this area."

The brothers and sisters responsible for various departments of the bruderhof are allowed to make routine decisions on what to do and on how much money to spend. But for bigger, unusual expenses they ask the steward's opinion. And if he is not sure either, the matter is talked over with the Servant of the Word or the Elder. It is not a case of one person ruling over the other or of building up a hierarchy. The various brothers and sisters have received a task from the community which they have to carry out. Of course, they can be questioned and can in a doubtful case be corrected by the community. Everyone knows that responsibility and authority can corrupt. Therefore, if the community feels you have not done justice to your task, you are given a different assignment.

Having to ask, having no rights, sounds very much like a lack of freedom. But we must not forget that all members of the community are responsible to one another. Nobody must decide in an authoritarian way according to personal feelings and impressions. Love is the stamp of their relationship to one another. Those who bear service functions don't rule but serve in the community. "As a steward or housemother one has a good opportunity to show love in practice. That is how I want to understand my task," one of them explains to me. "If somebody has to go to town and I give him the car key and money, I can also tell him to buy some ice cream for himself and also to take some home for his wife."

It is not only in little daily dealings that the community tries to live according to the Sermon on the Mount and the example of early Christian communism. They have turned away from anxiety for the future. There is no health insurance, no pensions, no life insurance, not even insurance against fire or accidents. "Here, too, we want to trust in God fully," they tell me. "Faith is not only an abstract ideal, but a matter of everyday life." In fact the only insurance the bruderhofs have is car insurance, which is demanded by law. If an accident occurs, however (as happened in 1957 when a big house went up in flames), they trust in the help of their sister communities and their Hutterian brothers.

By the way, there is no question about how much money the bruderhof has to spend for hair-cutting. It is Saturday morning and I walk through the workshop again. I stop short and take a closer look. Amazing! There, between half-finished baby high chairs and stacks of kindergarten tables, something like a portable barbershop has sprung up. Around a high stool are layers of various colors and textures. On the stool is seated an old gray-haired man, almost bald, ready to sacrifice a few of his not very plentiful hairs. This weekend task is accomplished in a manly way in the workshop. Shearing in a sheep pen must be similar.

The bruderhof hairstyle for men is short and flat at the sides—ears free, of course. But to compensate, the top is quite full and long. I applaud this service and money-saving chore to his neighbor by Andrew, today's "Servant of the Hair," as I call him.

On weekends everything here functions a bit differently. But isn't that true all over the world? The great sigh of relief, though, the escape into "weekend and sunshine," does not occur here, because the work of the week is felt to be so meaningful. On Saturday morning production in the shop goes on as usual, and during the present high demand for production some brothers work here even in the afternoon.

Elsewhere, the time after lunch on Saturdays is spent rather leisurely. The housewives bake their usual "sticky buns," "swirls," or "Jewish applecake" and refill their indispensable maple syrup. Some brothers mow the lawn and look after the flower beds on the small burial grounds of the community. Some have duties in the display room or sell community-grown tomatoes, beans, and watermelons at a roadside stand. Other typical weekend work is carwashing, fighting the algae on the pond, and preparation for Sunday.

There is a shalom meeting after supper and we are

invited. Vincent Harding, the black professor from Denver, will speak about the time of slavery and about the famous "underground railroad." It has little to do with a railway, but much with helping refugee slaves. In daring ways Christians helped to save slaves by means of underground passages and hidden cellar rooms. And they brought them to safety in northern America.

"Shalomer" is the name given here in Woodcrest and on the other bruderhofs to the unmarried members of the community. Their ages range from 18 to 50. The border is unclear, especially the upper limits.

I don't quite know what unmarried men and women have to do with the word "shalom," an Old Testament term for peace. This group is a good arrangement, though. They have their own choir and discussion groups. They hike together or take weekend trips. Surely many a bruderhof marriage was initially kindled on a shalom trip.

We are sitting with the Shalomers in a big circle in the dining room in the Rhön house. About eighty young people (more or less) are present. Above us hover four big fans bringing in the cool evening air. Cold shivers of expectancy cool the bare lower arms. It seems that these air whisks are always running. They probably also run in winter to bring the warm air down from the ceiling.

As I think back on this meeting, I remember my goose bumps and the impressive personal words of Vincent Harding.

For the bruderhofers who have grown up in America it has become clear to them again that immeasurable injustice has occurred in this country. All whites, they feel guilty and responsible toward this black man who explains to them the history of oppression and persecution of his race.

Some wipe away tears as they leave the meeting. Again in singing old slave songs they are obviously deeply moved. Bruderhofers are thin-skinned toward suffering and injustice. They feel for others and respond.

Later, when taking our usual evening stroll, we suddenly see torches flaming up behind the Pembrook house. There, under the flickering light, a large group of Shalomers have gathered underneath the windows of the guest rooms, where the Harding family is staying. In the dark, the sounds of old spirituals, with their solemn nostalgic melodies, filter over to us. They are a sign of thanks and of solidarity, of reconciliation and brotherhood, prayer songs.

We too receive a little treat, though of a different kind. Passing the Alm we notice a few people on the lawn in front of the house around a huge clumsy thing. It must be a whole family, barefoot children already in their nightclothes standing in line before a cylinder-shaped object. "Do you want to look through it?" they ask as we approach. "It's an especially beautiful evening tonight."

One of the Woodcrest schoolteachers had built a large telescope. Bruderhofers are enthusiastic astronomers and know the stars and their seasonal positions well. For the first time in my life I see the rings of Saturn and a few mighty moon craters in relief. Patiently I stand in line among small Hutterian boys and girls, barefoot and in nightclothes, waiting to have another look through the glass.

9

Haydn with Bean Salad!

Sunday! For many bruderhofers this is the most exciting day of the week. Something special is always going on, and the daily schedule is not so firmly fixed as usual. Preceding the worship service on a normal Sunday morning, there is a "Family Meeting." This is a relaxing half hour for everyone in the large dining hall with much singing and performances by the children's groups.

Today the preschool is performing an "original Bavarian clog dance." They are wearing "original Bavarian Tirolian caps," which were brought back from a trip, to nurture the German heritage. The little dancers hop around on the stage in a circle and intone "original German songs" laboriously peppered with a horrible "original American accents," to the general enthusiasm of all.

The bruderhof-German of the children is an interesting effort to hold onto the inherited language. But lacking much practice, it often remains more at the level of a humorous attempt. "Du bischt ein Fräschdäcks" (You're a rascal), the small daughter explains to me, for example, when I ask about her knowledge of German. She also knows "Faulpealz" (lazy fellow), "Ulkig" (funny), and "Fearkel" (piglet), and tells me about the princess on the "Aerbse" (pea). "The problem with German is that we always understand the things that we actually aren't supposed to hear," the neighbor's daughter tells us with amusement about the parents' attempts to keep secrets.

The Sunday Family Meeting is often followed by the *Gemeindestunde*. This is a Sunday worship service held outside on the village hill in good weather, and in the large hall in bad weather. Afterward there is time to play with the children, sit together with the guests, or go with the family down to the community burial ground, taking a few flowers to the graves of dear ones. Lunch is communal as usual and in the afternoon there is free time. Then some families take a drive with the horse wagon through the neighborhood, and sometimes invite their neighbors to ride along. Others go by car into the nearby Catskill Mountains, and Papa Maendel cycles with the oldest of his nine sons to go fishing in the Hudson River.

As everywhere else in the world one lets the soul relax on Sunday. A snack with coffee and pie sweetened with maple syrup helps the afternoon pass pleasantly. An enjoyable family supper is held outside, weather permitting. It includes abundant good-tasting homegrown tomatoes and the outdated Minute Maid fruit punch served straight out of the cardboard container from the Coca-Cola company.

Today, however, is a special Sunday. A festival hangs in the air. No, it's not for the wedding of Danny Moody in distant Manitoba. There for first time in bruderhof history, an old and a new Hutterite are marrying each other. This would be reason enough to celebrate. Nor is it because of the first baptism for a long time, which has just happened at the Darvell bruderhof in England and was transmitted by satellite and telephone line to all three American bruderhofs so they could enter into the experience. No, today it's a truly great day for the children! They have been looking forward to this event all week.

The children know that bags of candy will be handed out. There's not a lot of candy at the bruderhof. From time to time grandparents receive a ration of sweets to give to their grandchildren. Receiving candy on this special Sunday before school begins is a special treat.

The festive celebration is getting under way in the big dining hall. The schoolchildren sit next to their parents, proud of their new bruderhof blue shirts and skirts, which were introduced for all this summer. After a few songs a school play begins on stage with noisy fun. It has been prepared as an old-fashioned classroom. Four of the adult bruderhofers have dressed up as teacher and children to perform an improvised play. They are hardly recognizable.

As the play progresses, a dull student is filled with the ingredients of a brudferhof education with the help of a huge funnel. With an oversize drill an imaginary hole is made in this naughty boy's head. Large wood shavings (fresh from the factory) pour out of it, to the delight of all. Then the imaginary hole is thoroughly oiled and the funnel inserted. A couple of Webster's dictionaries and other old books are the first to disappear in the funnel. After a few oilings with maple syrup, a geometric triangle is tossed in and—according to the trend of the times—a couple of floppy disks from good Willy Wang.

At the end, however, the program becomes serious. Six first-graders tramp self-consciously down the center isle to the front. They stare longingly at the bags of candy stacked near the chalkboard. One after another they must show that they learned to write their names in preschool. They receive their treat only after successfully writing their names with screeching chalk. Then the new teacher is introduced. After receiving a gift, she marches with her class to the schoolhouse to introduce them to their classrooms and schoolbooks.

A little later the grown-ups follow. They want to see how things will be organized for the next school year. Who will sit beside whom and what schoolbooks will be used?

In front of the schoolhouse a couple of booths have been set up. In them are ice-cream cones and popcorn for all. In the school itself everything is spick-and-span—cleaned and decorated. Bright pictures hang on the walls. Student projects are exhibited. In the corner, the newly filled aquarium bubbles. Even the hamster has had his cage fresly polished. School at the bruderhof is a joyful community affair in which everyone takes part and rejoices.

Below in the extensive library new books and periodicals are on display. White-haired Edna tells me that I should definitely arrange to send her a new German Bible translation. Someone else shows me the new Peter Rabbit picture books, which are laid out in the section for the youngest children. The school is not off limits to the grown-ups of the bruderhof. This contact between all—the discussion of teaching techniques, the close working together between parents, teachers, and community—this is what creates the special character of a bruderhof education. Behind all this stands a carefully thought through educational philosophy which can be traced all the way back to Emmy and Eberhard Arnold.

Naturally, there are some discipline problems even in bruderhof schools. There are difficult and easy students, rowdy boys and "pious lambs." It is not thought that anyone should have a hanging head, though. A bit of wildness, daring, and enthusiasm for taking things on are expected. What counts most in the big and small happenings of the bruderhof children is the spirit in which they behave. Something that happens because of childish overenthusiasm or an immature lack of appreciation of values is passed over more casually than actions stemming from malice, envy, or jealousy.

The bruderhofers are quite down to earth with their punishment. Whipping is not permitted. Formal discipline ranges from short-term exile from the family and the community to transfer to a public school. That, however, is the rare exception. As a rule the bruderhof school is a pleasant educational environment, in which self-realization occurs simultaneously with education for community.

The liberal American school system is tolerant of the bruderhofs on these points. They are allowed to run their own school. No one prescribes an exact teaching plan. They can staff the school with their own teachers. Instruction can be shared by members of the community who haven't completed any teacher's training. Now and then written examinations are given to the pupils by the educational authorities, and at the end of the year report cards must be sent in.

The main concern is that after eight years of school a level must be reached which enables the students to keep up with their public high school counterparts. The bruderhofers apparently manage this easily. No wonder with the intensive and loving care offered here.

Naturally, there is a daily and weekly schedule—prepared with the help of colleague, Willy Wang. It includes seeing the sights of the bruderhof, as well as early morning physical training; a communal snack, as well as pottery-making or woodworking; projects on the grounds, as well as the more normal school subjects.

If the history lesson deals with evolution, the school-board-recommended history book is supplemented by reading a talk by Elder Heini Vetter, who said something on this issue five years ago in the Shalom group.

As soon as the theoretical part is done with, Ian and David disappear with some of the children to their special projects somewhere on the bruderhof grounds. As suggested in the text, they are making a fire without matches as was necessary in the Stone Age. The remaining five of the class in the meantime practice a spontaneous play about how the cave men made themselves understood without speech. In the background the aquarium bubbles away. In the glassed-in beehive, hardworking bees (an example to all) as a shining example, fly busily through the specially prepared tube in the window to their work outside. Truly the children are surrounded with lessons for head, hands, and heart. One would like to go to school again here.

The school grading reports are as carefully worked out and comprehensive as the lessons, on a pattern developed after many years of experience. Issued four times a year, the reports provide a careful evaluation of many areas of achievement and of behavior. This report card is an internal bruderhof grade, intended primarily for the benefit of the parents. A second official report is prepared for the public school board which contains only grades. The internal report card is blissfully free from pressure, taking away the fear of not passing. The average of three grades is reported in every subject. The report on English class may read 3-4-1/2.7.

The 3 reports on the inner influence of the student in the school. Does she work to support the group? Does she have respect for classmates and teachers? Does she help other students?

The 4 is concerned with the effort she exerts in the subject. Does she work hard, attentively, and punctually? Does she participate in the classroom? Does she ask when she hasn't understood something? Does she work willingly?

The 1 says something about the objective result. Did she understand what was taught, and what were the results of her work? The 2.7 is the average of the three grades. Only the latter is given to the state authorities. The best grade is 4, the worst is 0. So this sample grade tells us of a young bruderhofer who has a good attitude in English class, works really hard, but in spite of that doesn't grasp the subject very well.

Simultaneously with this evaluation, judgment is made by all the teachers on each student's readiness to help with practical work, contribute to a good atmosphere, and get along with classmates. Also considered are the breadth of the child regarding other children, the teachers, the community, and the world. Here again the help of Willy Wang appears to be needed, but if all goes smoothly it gives detailed information about the student.

In addition there is an attached page for longer comments from teachers and a space for the parents' responses.

One could easily imagine that so much analysis could lead to a "control neurosis." That is not the case, however.

The main approach to the students is love and the feeling that each one is a valuable gift to the community, and that each one deserves special care. School is not a world apart for the child. The parents are not far away. Daddy can be visited at his place of work, and Mama teaches biology. Big brother, who works in the wood factory, teaches turning plates on the lathe tomorrow morning. What should one be afraid of?

Only when they are thirteen or fourteen years old do the bruderhofers allow their children to go to public school. Later some go to college, or university for a specialized education. This period of distance from the bruderhhof, the slow adapting toward a self-reliant life at the university, is intentionally provided as an option for every young person. The bruderhof children should see the world and should be able to compare it to life in the community. They should become independent and capable of life outside, and only then freely decide the future they choose to embrace.

Nowadays many decide for the bruderhof life, but that was not always so. Again and again one meets parents with one or more grown children who have chosen to live outside the group. The more dynamic, enthusiastic, and attractive the bruderhof life is, the more likely the children will choose to join the community. But to become a member is also a question of a spiritual calling. Without a firm relationship to God it won't work out. Dependence, clinging to what one is accustomed to, or convenience are not enough to qualify one for life at the bruderhof.

The difference in public school, college, or university is obvious to the children. "At high school we don't call the teachers by their first names, you know," a fourteen-year-

The building where maple sap is boiled into syrup.

A festive occasion for the high school girls.

Grandma at the computer.

Sewing is done by the women.

There are always more clothes to wash and fold.

Rocking horses in the production line at the shop.

Josef inserting screws.

Cutting hair in the workshop.

. . . but the men do the dishes!

Communal harvesttime.

Communal sorting.

Bruderhof wedding art in the style of the German youth movement.

Family Meeting.

Outdoor snacktime in a scenic spot.

A little chat at the summer festival.

Worship meeting on the hill.

Encircling the lake.

Torches lead the way.

old tells me, who is in his first year at Kingston High School. "The teachers there are not really our friends as they are here."

At this phase of weaning from the bruderhof life, the demand for military service came up for the young men at the time of the Vietnam War—an impossibility for bruderhofers.

Resorting to violence does not go together with following Christ, for the Sermon on the Mount determines their quality of life. The only way out for the old Hutterites was often martydom, prison, or death. The bruderhofers, put on the spot, worked out something more bearable at the time of the Vietnam War, when young men were being drafted for military service.

In 1956 the Woodcrest Service Committee was founded as a beneficent organization. The government recognized it as providing acceptable alternate service opportunities. Certainly it wasn't possible for a Woodcrester to do his two years of service in Woodcrest—that would have been too easy. But Woodcrester young men of draft age were simply sent to the service committee of the New Meadow Run bruderhof in Pennsylvania, and the problem was solved. This convenient solution protected them from renewed emigration for their faith.

The big bell in its wooden roost in front of the archive building begins to ring. Two small bruderhof girls are hanging on the bell rope with skirts flying, swinging up and down to announce that it is time to go to lunch. Every bruderhof of the new Hutterites has such a bell—a new Hutterite specialty. The old Hutterites abstain from church bells just as they do from buttons on the men's black Sunday jackets. "Only the Catholics have those," they say. So with the bell the bruderhofers are somewhat Catholic, while without buttons they are good Hutterites. It took me two years to catch on that the community men always have snaps rather than buttons on their jackets. I still don't understand the background of this practice. Probably showy buttons are considered too decorative.

Everyone is streaming toward the Rhön house. The scene is especially striking today, since on Sunday most people wear brilliant bruderhof blue. In spite of the bell, I arrive late and must find a spare place somewhere between fully occupied tables. Aha, bean salad to enjoy. And what's more, Arnold Mason's distinguished and wonderful English-sounding voice says that today at lunch the summer section of Haydn's "Seasons" will be performed.

"Aha," I think, "for once they couldn't find something suitable to read aloud, so they will play a record." But Arnold Mason's announcement is hardly finished when the choir members stand up and march with soft footsteps (some again on bare feet) onto the stage. Quickly almost half of the places at the table are empty. As the Haydn summer storm breaks loose in the dining hall, the Sunday meal almost sticks in my throat. Only the bean salad, which continues to be comfortably spooned in by young and old with much clatter, keeps me from believing that I have been whisked away to the Vienna State Opera. As cold shivers run down my back, I stretch my neck and try to count. There must be nearly eighty singers. And what a sound! Haydn with bean salad! Good old Franz Joseph Haydn, like me, would probably rub his eyes in disbelief—and perhaps really enjoy the eager singers.

My lack of bruderhof experience is obvious in the fact that I can't digest Haydn and bean salad as fast as my refined neighbors at the table. They have continued shamelessly spooning their food at the usual bruderhof tempo, while my plate is still half full and the replenished serving bowl is already empty again. Well, it's reassuring that one can count on a snack in the afternoon!

Sunday always has some extra things to offer, but even on Sunday dishwashing and serving the tables are men's work at the bruderhof. Cooking and baking are up to the women. The other role expectations are more predictable. The men work in the shop, the women in household areas. The men plane, saw, and drill. The women wash, iron, and sew. Only in the offices and archives and publishing is there a mixed team. In spite of this, the women have equal rights as members of the community—even if they can't become Elder or Servant of the Word, which the community understands the New Testament not to allow. But the women are more self-assured and confident than many women in other religious circles. Certainly the reason has to do with the fact that the grown-ups all work here and no one is confined to one's own family and children. Each works for each.

Another somewhat hidden contribution toward feminine self-assuredness here is the fact that one receives one's "money" (the means of support) from the community, not the woman from the man, but all from each other.

In another area the women are not so liberated, or they hold quite unconsciously to a more reserved line. To be openly affectionate is rather uncommon at the bruderhof. Frequently I hear mention of this from other bruderhof visitors. To someone who comes from the outside, this is noticeable right away. Here one hardly ever sees a kiss, an embrace, or holding hands. Only quite young couples seem to shyly press one hand into the other, in an overflow of feeling, on their way to the dining hall. Unconsciously the visitor adjusts to this modest reserve. In so doing, he risks tension with his wife, who under the strain of living as guest is suffering a feeling of deprivation and is in need of a tender touch or a demonstrative holding of hands.

When spoken to about this, the bruderhofer reacts with surprise. "No, we have no special rules on this. Aren't we affectionate? That never even occurred to me," one of them tells me.

"Well, but it's not really nice when one does it too openly," Hela says. "What do you think?"

Apparently their reserve is almost an unconscious behavior code. "Perhaps they don't want to make it harder than necessary for the young people and the unmarried," I think to myself.

But certainly their modest attitude on sexual questions has something to do with it. This is a reserve which is not an inhibition. The bruderhofs are concerned with purity and modesty. Sex is not openly discussed. In school the subject hardly comes up. Young people are "officially enlightened" only shortly before their wedding. "The little children obviously are brought by the angels," my wife tells me after she has spent a morning with the preschool.

Contraceptives are not used. It seemed barbaric to Eberhard Arnold to prevent life in this way. "Souls are waiting in eternity to be called into life," Eberhard Arnold wrote regarding birth control in a book printed in the 1930s. But birth control is not necessary at the bruderhof. Children are wished for. There is room for big families and the families are well cared for. Faithfulness in marriage is assumed; divorce is not seen as an option. A sound, not cramped, but very reserved atmosphere rules in these things. Only—my wife thinks—they really could be a little more affectionate.

Household Meeting, *Gemeindestunde*, Brotherhood— that's what the different meetings of the bruderhof are called. This evening there is a Gemeindestunde, a service in which the members, the young people, and invited guests may all take part. The Brotherhood includes only the intimate circle of the members, sometimes with, and sometimes without novices. The Household Meeting, however, includes all inhabitants of the bruderhof.

We are invited to the Gemeindestunde. This evening (as is often the case in the summer) the meeting takes place on the hill at the edge of the village, near the water reservoir, in the manner and style of the earlier German youth movement. There is a wonderful view from here. My eyes sweep over the endless woods to the Catskill Mountains in the background.

Slowly the hillside fills up. The old people who can't climb the steep path anymore are brought up by car or on one of the many golf carts. We all sit on the ground in long rows under a couple of high trees. Only a few benches are provided for the older ones. The thick songbooks are handed out. Everyone sits in silent reverence, looking into the setting sun which is painting the sky with red and orange rays, as though ordered for the occasion. This is truly a romantic place. Above us shine the stars—electric to be sure—hanging gold and six-cornered from the trees (and, of course, homemade).

In front of me is the little cart from the dining hall on which are arranged several tape recorders and amplifiers, as well as a telephone. At that moment Gary jams a plug between the grass roots, and a moment later I hear a metallic crackling and roaring from the tree above me. Sure enough, even here in nature they have community with the other bruderhofs. The telephone line here on the hill allows the leading of the service and the sermon to come completely from the Deer Spring community today.

I hardly know how to conduct myself properly. On the one hand there is the romantic view of the brightly colored circle of kerchieved community people, who watch the exquisite sunset as they sit on this wooded hill. This makes one truly reverent. The quietness of the crowd adds to this. But somewhere behind me someone keeps saying, "Sh...!" Now also to my right someone says, "Sh...!" Who could that be. Otherwise, everyone is so quiet and attentive! Certainly the faces couldn't look more serious.

I notice that my wife next to me is shaking and has bowed her head. What is she giggling about now? This is certainly not a fitting moment! Embarrassing, very embarrassing! Quite ashamed, I look around, to see if anyone has noticed us. But again this, "Sh...!" Now I understand. It is the caring mothers with their disrespectful mosquito spray who are disturbing the contemplative silence. And to think that I had been intimidated by their spray cans!

But now the service begins, undisturbed and romantic. Powerful, solemn songs are sung. From far away through the telephone line comes the voice of the Servant of the Word in Deer Spring, who is reading a fitting word from Eberhard Arnold or some of the later elders. Someone in Woodcrest expresses his thoughts and what is important in connection with what was just read. Cool evening, beautiful songs, the sunset, the devout believers, who look with shining eyes into the wooded distance—everything breathes harmony and peace.

Obviously they enjoy this, and I begin to understand. In such hours they find the strength to continue, reflecting on the essential experience of community.

In spite of this, the bruderhofers haven't always had harmony. My thoughts wander back again. . . .

10

The Wilderness Years

What were the causes of the crises the community experienced between 1935 and 1962? The increasing estrangement from the Hutterians after 1950 was only a symptom. The problems of the bruderhofs went much deeper, and a part of the reason is as plain as day. Someone with the inner authority and discerning personality of Eberhard Arnold was lacking. His sons were too young at the time of his death to step into their father's shoes. Those who were entrusted with the leadership of the community depended more on their formal position than on their natural authority.

The Hutterian structures had their advantages, though. By the beginning of the fifties the community outwardly became much more peaceful. The threats to their physical existence were no longer there. They had settled down and their mind was again free to undertake something new. But this was fertile soil for the outbreak of both small and big conflicts, which till now had been buried or left in the background.

An important cause of the problems were the many new members who had not known Arnold nor experienced the beginnings of the bruderhof. Still more were unfamiliar with the program and ideas which motivated Arnold. Many who joined in England were pacifists. Caught in the crisis of their country, they wanted not only simply to say "No," but also sought for a meaningful alternative. The bruderhof, with its pacifistic stand and its life in community in which each served the others, seemed to them to be just right. But the spiritual motivation and the anchorage of their decision in faith were often less deeply embedded.

Whereas under Eberhard Arnold there was always a good balance between social work, care of the community, missionary engagement, and the spiritual life, these elements became more and more unbalanced in the community. Jesus Christ as the center point, decision-making through consultation with the Bible, and the leading of the community through the Holy Spirit, all fell more and more into the background. Instead, the community became an ideal for its own sake. Less and less did spiritual unity and consensus determine the course. A democratic majority began to take control.

A quotation from a fund-raising leaflet in 1952 clearly reflects this shift in the center of gravity:

> Everyone can live in community; you must only want it absolutely and give yourself completely to the community. Community means freedom—freedom from fear, freedom from disillusionments, from problems and destructiveness; freedom from self. Only community is the true calling of men, the fulfillment of their deepest longing.

The old crumpled tract, from which I take this quotation, has a handwritten note added later by a bruderhofer: "That sounds as if the word 'community' has replaced the word 'Jesus' as the center and goal of life." This is an appropriate analysis, but one which came too late. At first hardly anyone noticed that the ship of the community was torn away from its anchor.

Another bruderhof decision also symbolized the change of course. They wanted to gain new members and make new contacts. To make this easier, the barriers of the strict Hutterian forms were removed. At the same time, the center of their reason for being, their faith in Jesus Christ, became blurred. This does not mean that they ceased to be a Christian community. But little by little the center of gravity shifted from "Christian" to "community."

For an outsider it is extremely difficult after more than 25 years to separate cause and effect, and to presume to analyze accurately the significance of the great crises of the bruderhofs. Too many smaller explosions are mixed with larger trends. Inner spiritual motives are hard to correlate with outward circumstances. The bruderhofers themselves, looking back, see their difficulties originating from one great cause: the tension between two spiritual attitudes, two spheres of ultimate concern—the spiritual and the human.

"This fight is present and especially intense where the discipleship of Jesus unites people through God's Spirit to live in community. Through their lives in active peace, social justice, and joy in his Spirit, they give an open witness to the bankruptcy of Satan." So writes one of the oldest warriors of the bruderhof, Hans Meier.

"We are not at all surprised that such a life is constantly attacked from outside and from within through temptations. Our life brings with it an intensive spiritual struggle which from the outside becomes easily misunderstood as a human struggle for power and direction. It is not, however, the question which people should have power, but rather which spiritual power should rule!"

As with all bruderhof members, Hans Meier himself has experienced again and again how difficult it is to remain true to one's first calling. This is a clue to the origin of conflicts that smoldered in the community over many years.

The prospects for the bruderhofers looked good at the end of World War II. In the United States a strong community movement emerged which had a great interest in discovering convincing examples of established communities. In 1952-53, Heini Arnold (the second son of Eberhard Arnold) and his wife, Annemarie, were sent to the United States to respond to this newly awakened interest. Members of the Kingwood Community and the Macedonia Community were interested in the bruderhof and were considering whether they should join. In 1953 about half the Macedonia Community and almost all the Kingwood Community joined the bruderhof, a decisive milestone for the brudferhof, although at the time no one realized it. After this experience it seemed clear that a new bruderhof should be founded in the United States, since the community in Paraguay felt somewhat isolated, and long journeys were continually necessary to keep up contact with those in America or Europe.

Then in 1954 Woodcrest was founded, nearly 100 miles north of New York City—the bruderhof from which the community's new beginning would develop. The small Community Playthings enterprise which the Macedonia Community established, and brought with them to the new bruderhof, played a role in the development of Woodcrest that cannot be underestimated. The business developed by leaps and bounds, bringing what the bruderhofs had never had enough of before: money.

Soon it became clear that Heini Arnold was the natural leader for the new community. The contacts with interested Americans increased. Conferences were held at the bruderhof, and a steady stream of seekers came from nearby New York City. New members joined, especially from Quaker circles and the Church of the Brethren. The youngest bruderhof developed little by little into the most living shoot of them all. In 1955 there were already 150 people gathered in Woodcrest of which 30 were members and 15 novices.

An episode between 1954 and 1957 brought to a complete end the already cool relationship with the old Hutterians. Following the help given by five young carpenters from different Hutterite colonies with a building project in Woodcrest, the colony at Forest River expressed a great interest in drawing nearer to the bruderhof. But this wish for contact with the bruderhof was not done with the agreement of the rather isolated colonies in North Dakota. The fact that Forest River made overtures to relate to the eastern bruderhof without obtaining permission from the Hutterite elders offended them. Some families moved from the New York community to the Forest River colony; others moved from there to Woodcrest and soon felt united. Because of this, several old Hutterite families left Forest River under protest. And so a completely new bruderhof came into being, an unconsidered and arrogant action which led to a final break with the old Hutterites.

But in Paraguay changes were also taking place. New

bruderhofs were established—first in Uruguay, then also in Germany. As soon as the war was over, the bruderhofs had a great interest in the possibility of returning to Germany. In 1955 the community people were offered an estate in the neighborhood of their old Rhön location. The Sinn-talhof bruderhof near Bad Brüchenau in the Rhön was started. The leader was Hans Zumpe, who till then had been leader of one of the communities in Paraguay.

Other leading people from Paraguay moved to the communities in the United States, where there was more interest for the community and more life. Although with over 600 people, the majority of bruderhof members still lived in Paraguay, the base there became weaker and weaker. More and more the main activities took place far away from the bruderhofs in Paraguay. At first the communities there hardly noticed this shift of direction. Later awareness of this state of affairs began to grow until finally there was open discontent.

There were also problems in Forest River, the colony which had been "captured" from the Hutterians. The understanding grew that the way things had developed there had not been right. In addition, the families sent from Woodcrest found it difficult to adapt to the monotonous country life in the wide expanses of the prairie. They sought counsel with the other bruderhofs. After a nine-community conference in Paraguay at which most of the Servants of the Word were gathered, they gave the Forest River bruderhof back to the old Hutterians and moved away. To begin with, about ninety people lived in a rented hotel not far from Woodcrest. Then under pressure of time, they found what had formerly been a large hotel on the side of a lake in southwestern Pennsylvania. Thus the "Oak-Lake" bruderhof came into being, later known as "New Meadow Run." Many of the Forest River group are still at the bruderhof there.

But 1957 brought still more important experiences. After great inner struggles, the remaining members of the Macedonia Community joined. The Community Playthings enterprise became the complete property of the bruderhof. The big conference in Paraguay—recognized for the last time in this respect as the actual center of the bruderhofs—had one main concern. In planning for the future, they wanted to move a portion of the members to more densely populated areas of the world, where they could more easily sustain themselves. Again the main motivation came from Woodcrest. It appeared after this meeting that the inner leading of the movement actually shifted to the bruderhof in New York. Heini Arnold, together with some of the new American members there, developed a new vision. They wanted to regain the link to the old days of his father. They wanted to reestablish the spiritual roots of the movement.

Believing that the continued existence of the bruderhofs could only be secure through a clear inner attitude, they tried to clarify these matters at Woodcrest. They recognized that they had allowed too many guests and outside ideas to influence them. The extensive interaction with guests did not always have a positive effect on the community. The proximity to New York City and its modern society, with temptations and difficulties quite dissimilar from those in Paraguay, demanded a quite different approach by the bruderhof to protect its identity as a spiritual community. In the clarifying process they tried to put more time and energy into the care of the inner life and their spiritual motivations. Curious visitors were sent away. Only those whose inner attitudes were unambiguous were invited to interact with them. They had learned from the mistakes of the past.

In 1959 the long-smoldering crisis of the whole community broke out. Only the Woodcrest bruderhof remained essentially spared from difficulties. All the other bruderhofs fell into the most serious crises between 1959 and 1961. Almost all the leading members and Servants of the Word laid down their ministry, had it taken from them, or experienced a personal crisis. These conflicts struck deeper and deeper through every layer of the communities. The new generation of bruderhof children criticized the attitude of the parents whose lifestyle and ideal of community no longer appeared convincing. On the other hand, many of the older members criticized the new direction of the community and sought to hinder the progress there. Whole families left the bruderhofs in protest; others were sent away to find a renewal of their faith.

The Evergreen bruderhof (later called Deer Spring), which had been opened in 1958, also experienced a crisis. Many American members had found a home there. By the end of 1960 this bruderhof was closed for a time. Because of serious differences of opinion on the question of child education, further living together became impossible. At the beginning of 1961 the crisis in Paraguay came to a climax. The community in Primavera literally collapsed. Old conflicts broke out afresh, while long-suppressed personal difficulties were revealed. Hardly anyone understood clearly all the dynamics that were at play.

In February, at the invitation of the South American bruderhofs, a group of brothers led by Heini Arnold was sent by Woodcrest to Paraguay to help and advise in solving the problems. Many serious talks with all the members followed. A hard spiritual fight raged which eventually resulted in almost half the 540 people in the communities either being sent away or leaving of their own accord. But even that was not a final solution. At a certain point in the crisis the bruderhof was dissolved because they could no longer find a basis for a really united community. Soon after this unanimous dissolution, a new bruderhof was founded drawn from former members. Twenty, mostly younger people, formed the core group with which a new beginning could proceed. Soon many of the former members of the community joined again.

By the end of 1961 the crisis was over. All the bruderhofs in South America were dissolved. Also the new community in Germany and one of the English bruderhofs no longer existed. Nearly half the members of the community had left the bruderhofs or had been sent away. The remaining members lived at the three American locations, or at the English Bulstrode-Hof. The latter was also given up in 1966 in order to concentrate themselves geographically in the United States to enhance their unity and facilitate working together.

Because of the very large size of the communities, their inadequate supervision, separate development, openness to outside influences, and the loss of their spiritual identity, the bruderhofs faced the greatest crisis of their history.

But a new beginning was made. They found their way back to the early Christian community model, with Christ at the center of their life, in a living relationship with God. In 1962 Heini Arnold was elected elder and leader of the three bruderhofs. He who more than anyone had led them out of their crisis would be the one to lead them into the future. The community had returned to the vision of its founder Eberhard Arnold. A new healthy moving forward started, and by 1963 over 200 of the earlier members had returned to the bruderhof.

An earthquake had shaken the bruderhofs. Everything had been changed in the turmoil. A new commitment was made to the "old" standards, to the "old" identity. New unity was sought for. The community was experiencing a spiritual rebirth. It had to recover like a plant bent by the storm, establishing strong roots and healthy shoots before it could again face outside influences.

What followed as a consequence was a clear-cut separation from the outside world. Almost all contacts with other communities were dissolved, the working together with other groups and movements reduced. Concentration on the essential reality was emphasized now. This situation also explains the focusing of attention on the teachings and thoughts of Eberhard Arnold, which is obvious to visitors even today. In a counterreaction to the crises and false ways, which had started with the rejection of Arnold and his way of thinking, they delved ever more into his heritage and began to investigate it and make good use of it. Books of his sermons were published. Many of his mealtime addresses which had been taken down in shorthand were transcribed and translated into English. His letters and diaries were combed for wisdom.

Also a way back to the Hutterians opened up. Here was a source of stability, a long tradition of community experience. That was important to them again. These contacts must be rebuilt. The first attempt at reconciliation with the Hutterian brothers took place in 1964. A journey to Manitoba was undertaken, and forgiveness was requested for taking over the Forest River colony.

One of the few enterprises which the bruderhof tackled at this time outside the community was to lend their support to Martin Luther King. Several members traveled to the South and took part in marches with the black civil rights people.

But still no final inner peace came to them. Only the financial situation appeared good. Community Playthings grew and flourished. Not until 1967, after the closing of the last English community, can we speak of the bruderhofs finally achieving real peace. There was good contact between the three communities in the United States, and together they could build up something new. Still more former bruderhofers returned and were accepted as full members with all privileges and responsibilities.

Joint conferences were held. At one of these meetings of all the communities in 1971, it was decided for the first time since the great crisis to open a new bruderhof. Once again the way led back to England, where since 1971 the Darvell bruderhof in East Sussex has existed. A strengthened contact with the Hutterians also began to show itself. Elders and preachers visited from the colonies. In February 1974 the Hutterian Brethren accepted the bruderhofs back into their fellowship. As a representative of the Eastern communities, Heini Arnold had in great humility asked for forgiveness for all the dividing and hurting actions of the past. For their part, the Hutterian Brethren of the West offered a renewed and complete uniting. Kerchiefs and Hutterian costume were accepted again in the Eastern communities.

But the inner significance of this reuniting was much greater than the outer changes. They had regained their connection with the centuries-old stream of Hutterdom—fellow Christians whose faith and life stood nearest to their own. The will to community had conquered over the constantly driving power which had caused them to become lost in individualism and isolation. The bruderhofs had also found their way back to the old vision of Arnold, who had given so much strength and energy for joining with the Hutterians. The Spirit of God, who wants to gather and unite, had conquered.

Again and again larger and smaller crises occurred. But the community as a whole was no longer brought into danger. The relative isolation from the surrounding world was bit by bit also loosened again. Contacts with other communities began anew; journeys and visits were made; work with prisons was started.

On July 23, 1982, Heini Arnold died. The son of Eberhard had led the bruderhofs back to the vision of his father, and had brought about reuniting with the Hutterites. The loss of Heini was in itself a strain on the community.

Heini's son Christoph was temporarily appointed as new elder, and in 1983 confirmed in this role. Once again struggles for power and leadership took place. But the direction found under Heini Arnold of inner stability and the new opening to the outer world was pursued. The community recognized its need to give a constantly united and clear witness, to maintain clean motives, to live a correct lifestyle, and to give up everything daily anew to God and to one another.

At the end of 1983 the bruderhofs decided to lower their standard of living to free more money for service to others. They determined not to be bound to the success of their well-run business and to renew their efforts toward bringing their witness to the outside world.

It is clear from the history of the bruderhofs that no one on the bruderhofs can foretell their future. Will they return to Germany one day? Will new crises shake the community? As they move into the future, human strength is not reliable, and human will power not adequate. Changes happen quickly on the bruderhof. The community is on its way through history—out of the many hundreds of wills and lives to form one will, to find one way together. Who knows where they will be tomorrow?

Those who visit a bruderhof will scarcely be aware of these crises and struggles. The bruderhofers do not peddle their problems abroad. Also, the Hutterians are not exactly talkative about the difficulties in their history. This book is the first publication to speak with the support of the community about the various historical backgrounds of the bruderhofs. Even here some things are mentioned only in a general way. Many details and names, many themes and problems, are consciously withheld.

And that has its reason. If there is to be forgiveness, they must "forget." No community will endure if again and again the failures of different ones are stirred up, uncovering past guilt, and revealing scars made by earlier mistakes. New ways can be taken only when the old relationships are fully purified. Forgiveness on the bruderhof means full acceptance and receiving again—not being looked at askance, but being an equal among equals.

Almost every member of the bruderhofs has experienced problems. Many have left the community for a time, considering themselves serious failures. Servants of the Word, stewards, work-distributors, housemothers, teachers, office workers—persons in all of these roles have been removed from their positions because they have denied their calling, or have gone in wrong directions. But after having recognized their errors, they have all been taken back.

Again and again human behavior, envy, egotism, jealousy, and striving for power overtake the spiritual view of things. But once again repentance and forgiveness restore persons to a useful place in the community. Without this very specific "ecological" balance, the community would quickly die. But because each one knows his own weaknesses and dangers, his own failure, his own repentance—for this reason the failures of others are also forgotten and as far as possible never brought up again. But this also makes it difficult for a chronicler to write an exact history of this community.

The curious will not be satisfied—either through a visit to the bruderhof or through this book. But to forgive, forget, and find restoration of our spirits is important for us also who do not live on the bruderhof or in a community.

11

Festivities for All

"**D**o you have *Spiessbraten* in Germany?" is the most frequent question we've been asked the past few days—always with a twinkle in the eye. When I answer that of course I know *Spiessbraten*, because it is a German word, they stare at me in unbelief. *Spiessbraten* at this bruderhof involves anticipation and promises festivity. *Spiessbraten* here refers to their annual summer festival down by the pond, the social climax of the year, one might say. The joyful anticipation on all sides naturally arouses our expectations. Summer festival with the Hutterians? How can one adequately describe it?

Obviously, this time it has something to do with the homecoming of Christoph Arnold, who is returning today from the baptism in England. So it is also a "welcome" celebration. Festive as the bruderhof life is, before the big celebration there is first to be a small one. We must get ourselves ready for the imminent welcome. Celebration Part I begins.

Gradually we are becoming accustomed to how such

things work out. The driver who has brought Christoph and his wife, Verena, from John F. Kennedy Airport stops just this side of New Paltz. He telephones to announce how near they are to arrival. The word is passed quickly around and the activities of the whole community are brought to a standstill. Everyone turns out—the shop brothers down on the bend, the women and children and office workers. All line the road up toward the village. Songs are sung, hands are waved. Everyone is in a festive mood.

At half past three as we come down the steps of the archives, everyone is already gathered outside. Most people are waving the traditional bruderhof blue. The children are waving homemade flags, and the preschool has made a huge welcome sign. The bruderhofers stand so close together that one has to crane one's neck to see the arriving couple. Yes, there they are, actually arriving! The old familiar Dodge rolls slowly up the road. Songs ring out. Flags with the yellow-orange burning heart emblem of the bruderhofs wave vigorously. Blue shirts press forward toward the road, the breast pockets decorated with the burning heart symbol clearly visible!

This outpouring of emotion reflects the genuine joy of sharing in the homecoming of a brother and his wife. Christoph is just a normal Hutterite bruderhofer dressed in sneakers, and suspenders, with a beard and welfare-type spectacles. Now there is embracing and shaking of hands. The day has had its high point. Woodcrest is once more complete!

Christoph Arnold has been elder of the four new Hutterian bruderhofs since April 1983. He is a young elder, I would judge between forty and fifty years old. The communities learned in the tumultuous years of their history

that good leadership is important. One elder for all the bruderhofs can contribute more to the communal development and the life of spiritual unity than four equally strong
elders on four separately developing communities. Since
the appointment of Heini Arnold in 1962 they have
learned much in this area from their own history.

The role of elder is not a matter of exercising power over
others. The elder is first among equals. He represents the
members of the community in relating to the outside world
and in moving toward their agreed-upon goals. Just as the
elder has to be appointed and confirmed by all, so he can
also have the assignment taken from him if it is felt by all
that he is not functioning effectively.

But the elder is not the only one who is entrusted with
the tasks of leadership. There is a whole structure of
administration. Each bruderhof has two, three, or four
"Servants of the Word," a kind of pastoral ministry for the
spiritual welfare of members of the community. In addition to these servants, there are about six "witness
brothers," all men, who help the Servants in various tasks
of daily leadership. Supporting the six witness brothers on
the women's side are about six "housemothers"—often
wives of the Servants—with responsibility for coordinating
housekeeping and the domestic life of the community, as
well as the spiritual care of the women and girls.

Although the duties of the leaders above include
spiritual matters as well as practical ones, the main tasks of
the steward and work-distributor are limited more to material things. The steward functions as a kind of business
manager, the work-distributor as a personnel manager.
Each work department—shop, kitchen, archives, publishing—in turn has its own work manager who is responsible

for the inner organization of the department. In spite of such a hierarchy of duties, they remain brothers and sisters equally responsible to each other spiritually, contributing to the mutual good of everyone in the community.

But bruderhofers are ordinary people with normal emotions and weaknesses. Again and again annoyances and dissatisfactions crop up. The need for good leadership is indisputable, and is confirmed through the witness of the New Testament, the Hutterian Brethren, and the experience of their own communities. The bruderhofers say that community without leadership does not function, and that leadership without true community is not effective either. Nobody here wants to lord it over others. Rather, they want together to let themselves be ruled by the witness of the Bible and the Spirit of God. The leadership structure of the bruderhofs must, on behalf of all, simply watch over and promote this common good. The members each know their weaknesses, their willingness and unwillingness, and are open to warning and criticism given as a positive help in the life they have entered together. Leadership on the bruderhof does not have the negative aftertaste of the worldly hierarchy and use of power, but is a simple recognition of mutual admittance of human inadequacy.

The homecoming of Christoph Arnold is not the only high point of the day. We experience now an event which, considering how bountifully blessed with children the bruderhof is, likely has become almost routine for members of the community. After supper Winifred takes us by the arm and tugs us along in the stream of bruderhofers which is headed for the "mother house," a middle-sized building on the left side of the village.

The mother house is something like a hospital and maternity home rolled in one. Here bruderhofers who are very sick and need intensive nursing are cared for. But here also the mothers and newly born babies, just returned from the Kingston hospital, are housed together with their husband and fathers for two weeks after the births. In this way the family has quiet and time to adapt themselves to the new situation, and to concentrate completely on the tiny offspring. Recognizing that the daily activities of the community must proceed continuously, the mother house is a sheltered sanctuary of quietness.

Winifred explains to us that this procession supports the goal of preserving the quiet of the mother house. Naturally, every bruderhofer wants to see and scrutinize the new baby, to decide who he takes after, whether he has any hair on his head, and whether he looks around and is plump and healthy. With 400 curious visitors, that would cause a continual disruption. So a fixed time is arranged for a general viewing.

If only one could write musical pictures—for what awaits us at the mother house can hardly be described in words. Imagine the warm summmer evening air of the bruderhof, the high trees, the soft evening twilight, the chirping of crickets, and fireflies floating by. Add to this heavenly choirs of angels! Yes, choirs of angels! For as we arrive at the mother house we see the brothers and sisters standing in a long line in front of the window, and we hear them singing again. How they are singing! Appropriate old-world cradle songs! And all under the gentle evening sky.

I stand in the middle of it all, gradually moving forward with the line until I can see the display window. There stands the family—the radiant mother, the proud father, the self-consciously proud brothers and sisters. They stand and accept the ovation, just like living shop window dolls. Candles are burning on high stands. The children and the baby are wearing long white artistically embroidered gowns. The baby wears a flower garland. It's a living group portrait from great-grandma's photo album. The event is beautiful, moving, strangely intimate and unspoiled.

By Saturday morning the annual summer festival is drawing near. Early in the day, Danni is already enthusiastically starting to transform the huge quantities of meat, freshly delivered by the steward, into genuine bruderhof *Spiessbraten* (beef grilled on skewers). *Spiessbraten* in Woodcrest! That is quite a different matter from when the housewife grills a pound or two of meat on the stove at home.

Simple and modest as the food usually is here, at the summer festival one may really indulge! The bruderhof grill is of community proportions. An old ten-thousand-liter oil tank has been split lengthwise by the bruderhof's ingenious metalworkers. This huge pan, mounted on a tractor trailer, serves as a mobile barbecue grill. A roaring fire has been kindled from scrap wood from the workshop. By early afternoon as we arrive at the pond, the traditional spot for the summer festival, a spicy aroma floats over the water.

Little by little the whole bruderhof arrives. The old folks are brought down by horse and wagon, while the young ones walk. The area around the pond looks like a recreation park. On the jetty a few grandpas are passing the time fishing with their grandsons. On the left side of the pond the grill is smoking away by itself. A large plastic container of ice water stands there for refreshment. Dick, Don, and Danni invite us first to sample the meat. They stand there pleased to hear complimentary remarks made about the special taste of the meat prepared Paraguayan-style.

"In Paraguay we grilled over a large hole in the ground," Danni tells us. But not only meat is offered for tasting.

"Would you like a beer?" asks Dick slyly with raised eyebrows.

"Yes—uh, do you have beer?"

"Come with us," they say, grinning. And sure enough, not far from the great Hutterite grill, in a protective thicket at the edge of the wood, alone and secluded stands a barrel of beer. It is already tapped.

"There you are. We haven't exactly hidden it," the three hasten to explain. "It is only here because of the children. They must not be led astray."

Meanwhile those who are gathering have begun to play games—the older children on one side of the pond, the younger ones with their parents and grandparents on the other. In a huge circle they are playing drop the handkerchief with several handkerchiefs and several runners.

A little later, when the first supply of games has run out and the children's excitement has cooled a bit, everyone forms a huge circle around the pond for a grand march. The whole community—400 souls—march hand in hand around the water!

When it is time to eat, they again form a large circle and a song is sung. Then we each take our turn at the buffet. The delicacies are laid out on long tables. Each one gets his portion of *Spiessbraten*, fruit punch, salad, rolls, hot dogs, strawberries with cream, and much more. Now and again one of the men disappears into the wood where the "barrel of temptation" stands, and fetches a second draft—in moderation, of course. One small barrel for a hundred men, that is just truly for fun!

I sit in the circle and look around. All these faces have now become familiar to me. Many of them I know by name, especially the older ones. These are people whose life stories could fill books. To my right Trudi and Walter are sitting. Trudi has been with the bruderhof almost from the beginning. Sometime in the early twenties she came as teacher to the bruderhof in Sannerz. She is the community's walking history encyclopedia. She knows all the young people well and taught many of them at one time or other.

Next to her on the left is her husband, Walter, a genial Swiss. His route to the bruderhof began as a child. At Zurich he saw trains filled with prisoners and with wounded soldiers of the First World War. He could hear the cries of the wounded all the way to his home. He never forgot that. Participation in war was not possible for him. Later in a Quaker group in Paris, he found an article about Eberhold Arnold and the young community in Sannerz. He set out for Sweden to take part in the adult education classes there. But on the way, he got stuck at the Sannerz bruderhof. Stories and histories!

On the slope diagonally opposite, Franzi and her husband are sitting. He was a native of Scotland, she an Austrian Jewess. Dick studied for six years in a Catholic seminary for priests. Then he broke off his training, became a street sweeper in Edinburgh for the duration of the war, and eventually found the bruderhof. With the help of a friend, a daughter of Sigmund Freud, Franzi escaped from Vienna. Franzi, an energetic and lively person, has just learned to type and is working in the archives. She is one of the many grandmothers at the computer who in their old age are mastering new technology.

Next to them is another of the original older couples who learned to know each other on the bruderhof and give a special flavor to this community—Joseph and Ivy Stängl. He is a baker lad from Bavaria, she a graceful Scottish woman in whom one still senses the charm of the south of France, where she grew up. Joseph arrived at the bruderhof as a tramp.

"Most of the tramp boys like me only stayed for one day because the food was so poor," he explains. But Joseph was gripped by the naturalness, openness, honesty, and glowing warmth of Eberhard Arnold. True, he found the food on the Rhön terrible, even compared with what he got on the country roads. But as a trained baker he could make an important contribution to the community. At first he wanted to stay only for a short time. Then he decided to stay a bit longer. Finally he remained for good and now the community had its own baker.

Ivy's father was a pacifist, a professor of medicine, an adventurer, and above all, a free thinker. As a Scot he went voluntarily to France determined to improve international understanding. As a child Ivy belonged to a group which could be compared to the German youth movement. She encountered the bruderhof purely by chance through an article in the London *Times*.

The younger generation can also contribute stories. George tells how as a volunteer in the U.S. Army, he took part in much evil after the war in the Philippines. He describes the devastated cities there, the poverty, and how he had to stand guard on the city's trash dump to keep starving children from stealing rotten food. One day a child was shot there. That made him a pacifist. Afterward he tried a number of communities, but nothing came of it until he arrived at Woodcrest by way of the Macedonia community.

There is Carroll, who was a government official, and there is Doug, who sat in prison in World War II as a conscientious objector. And Dick, who a few years after the conflict, cycled with his wife through war-ravaged Germany seeking reconciliation. After their return home, imitating Thoreau, they went to the woods. They built themselves a log hut, and lived there for four whole years. Later by way of various other communities they arrived at the bruderhof.

Or I think of Charles, whom we met at the Deer Spring bruderhof. He came for a visit to the Cotswold bruderhof in England through his brother. The people there were so friendly and warmhearted that he burst into tears at the farewell. He had never experienced anything like it.

"I am the type of person who does not show feelings like that," he explained. "But I was so overcome that the bruderhof did not leave me in peace. I came again and again."

In the end he joined, and his first job was to set up an accounting system for the community.

"Man alive! Their bookkeeping was in such a muddle—all at sixes and sevens!" he told me in his charming English-accented German. To this day, forty years later, he can't get over it.

Or there is a one-time pastor in the Church of the Brethren whom I also met in Deer Spring. "I got fed up trying to convince Christians that they should be true

Christians," he told me. He left his church and with his wife came to the bruderhof. Now he works in the shop.

People on the bruderhof—stories, destinies, turning points. People—that is the actual treasure here. People who have risked something for their faith, who in order to live like the early Christians have broken away from conventional lives and careers.

All these life stories are surrounding me. I know some things about them, but still so little. I know their conversion stories, but so little of their immediate problems and difficulties. I am intimate with them, and yet they live in another world which is not my world. Could I live like this? Do I want to live like this?

All around me the festival goes on. We are singing again—songs of the youth movement which came into disrepute in the Nazi era and mostly fell into disuse. Here they are not burdened with these associations. Their songs resound with joy in four-part harmony as always. The history of the bruderhofs flows in a straight line from the 1922 favorite *"Früh tau zu Berge"* ("To the Mountains in the Dewy Morn") to "Und wieder blühet die Linde" ("The Lindens Are Blossoming Again") in 1984.

I have no sooner thought this, than someone stands up and tells us that in the early days on the Rhön they celebrated summer solstice with a fire, and while singing fire songs jumped through the flames. One of the men goes over to the other side of the pond and sets fire to a huge pile of wood. Immediately the special "fire song" books are handed out. The whole community walks over to the other shore, forms a circle, and sings fire songs from the German youth movement. The flames leap high, and slowly the pile of wood sinks down.

The final march is launched in an unusual manner. Six or eight Shalom boys approach the fire carrying large torches which they kindle there and light the trail through the woods and along the cornfield back to the village. The festival has ended. The long column of the community's men, women, and children stretches out in a colorful procession toward home. It is a beautiful sight—at front the torches flaring in the twilight, behind the long, many-colored line of old and young.

12

A Bruderhof Balance Sheet

Not only celebrations come to an end. Also our time on the bruderhof will soon be over. As it was with the Hardings a few days ago, we shall also receive a farewell. A farewell here almost borders on bribing one to come back again, or better still, to stay and join the community. Half the village will throng together, and songs will be sung. I will again shake hands with women in black kerchieves, and embrace stubbly graybeards. The door of the car will close as the wistful farewell song, "Till We Meet Again," brings a lump to my throat. I know already that I will likely feel something akin to homesickness. Homesick? Is this my home? Could I actually live here?

How often I have asked myself that question! Fascination and attraction have alternated with feelings of strangeness and distance. Nearly every evening I went to bed wondering. Could I live like this? Give up everything? My time, my property, my will? I weigh the advantages and disadvantages of this life, wavering between enthusiasm and criticism, considering the good and the bad. I strike a balance, listing the debits and credits. A table of positive and negative points take shape in my head.

In many ways, I am enthused, moved, and convinced. I admire their radical lifestyle, the complete surrender to their convictions, their absolute reliance on the words of the Bible, their simple faith in God. It is a faith with deeds as well as words. There is a genuineness to such Christianity that I long for myself, a way of life that convinces me. Nothing lukewarm, compromised, or half-baked— qualities I know only too well in myself. Their faith bears witness to the absolute power of God which upholds them. A faith not dependent on human motivation. A faith which shatters the rigid framework of traditions, structures, timetables, and fixed dates. A faith which comes to life, moves them to action, and does not bog down in endless Sunday sermons and appeals.

The love among these people is tangible. Their efforts to understand and accept me go far beyond sympathy or antipathy. No doubt they sometimes experience anger, envy, jealousy, and quarreling. But I saw nothing of that during our visit. I heard no bad words. I met no rejection and encountered no impatience. I have observed sound families, sound marriages, and sound relationships. I saw hardly any evidence of conflict between the generations. Young and old are of one heart and one soul. They are moving together toward the same goal. The older members are living the life that the younger ones wish to live. They admit their weaknesses, do not feel superior, and take one another seriously. Seldom have I seen such reverence and respect shown to the elderly. Seldom have I seen people who inspire such reverence and respect as here.

The place radiates an atmosphere of peace, security, and

love. Nonviolence is not only a slogan for peace demonstrations but for everyday life. Forgiveness, honesty, and directness—forgetting the wrongs done to one another are all practiced daily. Human relationships are important here; people are valued more than things. To be is more important than to have. Quality not quantity, deeds not words, love instead of competition—one could write a long list. Much cannot be expressed in words—it's an atmosphere, a spirit.

However, there is also the other side. Their way of life is different, unfamiliar, in some ways incomplete, and complicated by human elements. All of this must be mentioned when striking a balance.

What pains me most about the community—however, this might be explained by their history—is a lack of an essential legacy of Eberhard Arnold's witness and of the revival movement of that time. The bruderhof has gathered and many have come—but too few are sent out. Simply keeping the community functioning claims too much time, strength, and effort. Most members work at the maintenance and upkeep of the community. The major effort is directed to wood and metal instead of to people who are seeking longingly the meaning of life, and need to see this example and learn about it.

The people of the bruderhof are like coins in a treasure house. The treasure house may be inspected. There are guides. The luster of the gold may be admired. But the money remains inside. The life that could speak to so many is located outside the danger zone where it is desperately needed. The city on the hill is not to be overlooked, but life runs its course within its walls. It is not easy to benefit from its insights. Pacifism, community of goods, love, trust in

God—these are a mighty sharp thorn in the flesh of the world, but the flesh is too distant from the thorn!

On the other hand—who am I and where do I come from that I should attack with such sharp words? How do I myself live? How do the Christians in my own Central Europe live in the fortresses of their churches, through whose wide-open doors so seldom anyone looks in? What are we presenting to society with our Christian lifestyle? While the bruderhof has something to show, our empty churches and barren traditions hardly have anything to say to anybody—even if someone unexpectedly has an interest in it.

The bruderhofs convey a united whole, a genuine model of Christianity. Our own churches are constantly quarreling and fighting over theological distinctions while the members can do almost anything they like.

The Christians of Central Europe live in the midst of the world. Maybe we are even visible—but our thorn is blunt and does not even provoke opposition anymore. Perhaps we have become so lukewarm and indifferent because we have mingled so intensively with a lifestyle that always clamors for more, and better, and greater material things. We have been absorbed in wanting something for ourselves, instead of being something for others. We have become nondescript Christians, easily taken for any other honest citizen. The salt that we should be, according to the Sermon on the Mount, has lost its strength.

But salt does not only lose its function because it has become lifeless. Even pungent, serviceable salt can lose its purpose—if it remains in the salt cellar! The best salt is of no use if it is not put into the world's soup. Fortunately the members of the bruderhof are becoming increasingly conscious of this in recent years. They are waking up. A new phase is dawning. Following the inner strengthening and consolidating of the community, there is once again a more vigorous outreach toward the world.

But understandably there are fears to overcome. "New outlets?" they ask. "Wouldn't that be dangerous for us? Will we be able to retain our identity? Will we be able to cope with the dangers to which we expose ourselves? Haven't we paid a price for that already in our history? Isn't maintaining our community—with our families, children, and work—worthy in itself? Might the new destroy our unity?"

These are justifiable fears. New directions will be able to develop only slowly. But the God who has steered them securely and safely through a confused century, will also give them the wisdom to deal with these problems.

The bruderhofs struggle with the danger that the community itself can at times seem more important than Christ. Haven't certain elements crept into the community that cause the unrivaled importance of Jesus to be doubted? These must be dealt with.

In the early years under Eberhard Arnold the community overflowed with visitors. Thirty people hosted 1,000 guests. Today the proportion threatens to be reversed with 1,000 community members relating to thirty guests. Moreover, conferences, workshops, and efforts toward mission are not everyday occurrences as they were at the time of Eberhard. The first fire has gone out. But these problems are acknowledged by the bruderhofs. They are setting out; they are on the way. Perhaps they must tell themselves again and again that their security does not depend on leadership, however good. Nor in plans, however well thought out. But only in the God who has preserved them till now and who will also carry the future risks of their journey.

Few visitors will be able to overlook the significance Eberhard Arnold has for the community. To this day, his books, sermons, after-dinner talks, his answers to questions, and his example are given high priority at the bruderhofs. His theological approach, his responses to world issues or to problems of communal living, his understanding of the Bible and of biblical exegesis pervade the daily life of the communities. In Arnold and in the teachings of the early Hutterites they find inspiration for their practical day-to-day life. Arnold's strong commitment to mission has not yet been recovered to the same extent. To some it may seem as though they read the Bible through the eyes of their founder or their Hutterian forefathers.

This overemphasis can best be explained by considering what happened since the death of their founder—the danger and pain they have gone through whenever they have strayed from the original path to follow new ideas of their own! It was their need to recapture the past, to rediscover Eberhard Arnold, that brought about this strong leaning toward the witness of the forefathers. At the same time the bruderhof members know full well that the Bible alone protects from false ways and self-made ideologies. They acknowledge that only a living contact with the Bible can give correction and leading for a sound community life. So in recent times, God's Word is once again coming to the fore. Here, too, there are new developments, there are changes.

The particular emphasis on Eberhard Arnold is complemented and even imperceptibly fostered by the relatively unimportant place theology has at the bruderhof. In the United States the word theology has a rather negative connotation, one that denotes dry discussions and hollow phrases. . . .

Yet a clean theology, with down-to-earth statements about God and faith, can free one from human dependence and undergird a life of faith. At the bruderhof, however, theological knowledge is inherited rather than studied. There is no formal preacher training. Former theologians are today sanding rocking horses.

But the churches in my own country of Germany don't have much help to offer the bruderhofs. Theology and life seem to have little to do with one another. Deep personal convictions are seldom found. Structures, forms, and traditions have often stifled spiritual life. But the answer to our situation is the same answer as for the bruderhofs. Genuine life, clear direction, and daily renewal are not found through form and tradition but only at the source itself. Without personal continuous listening to God's living Word to us, without genuine relationship to him, life is stifled.

A stumbling block for every outsider is the distinctive costume, along with the peculiar and arbitrary character of the Hutterian way of life. The significance of the inner unity for the life of the community can certainly not be overestimated. But the fact that the inner unity should demand so much outward conformity seems to me tough to accept. It is a very high price that the Eastern communities pay for unity with the old Hutterians. Costume and tradition build up quite a few additional hurdles for outsiders. The "offense of the cross" is augmented by the "offense" of conformity to outward form. Well—that is their personal style of discipleship and one could say that whoever is put off by these outward forms has grasped very little of their inner life.

However, even the inner aspect of their concept of unity preoccupies me. Without inner unity, often nothing is undertaken. If disunity reigns, the strength to act is missing. The bruderhofs have a good point. Churches such as mine, in which ministry to peace may be "with weapons or without weapons," in which one may be either active or passive, rich or poor, charismatic or mission oriented, left or right—in which just about anything and everything seems possible—is not exactly a convincing arrangement.

But can full unity ever be really attained? And what is unity? Something emotional, fleeting, that comes and goes, which I sense or feel the lack of? Or is it the implicit, deliberate will to hold onto goals held in common? Can unity be achieved through human agreement, or is it a gift of God? Can there not be unity in spite of differences of opinion? Is it even possible in our humanness to experience unity except for brief moments? In any case, should one not act? When there are urgent problems, is it right to wait until a group feels completely united?

It seems to me that true unity is either never possible, because we all have many weaknesses and faults, and never attain the "golden moment"—or unity is always possible, in spite of our weaknesses, because it is simply a matter of mutually embracing a common goal. Do you have to wait for unity before taking action? This basic conviction of the bruderhof is a problem for me. However, lacking convincing alternatives, I also have no answer.

It also seems questionable to me whether subjection to the will of God must always include subjection to the will of the community. True, no one is compelled by the community. The pattern of assent, the concept of unity, sees to that. Each one has to agree individually on important matters, or the decision is postponed. But is it not possible in daily life, through human weaknesses for something to creep in that makes the individual needlessly bend to the common will? Will not many a decision almost be imposed on the group. Is each one truly in agreement with everything—or simply too tired to contradict after a long day's work? That not everyone is able to represent equally the decisions of the community is proved by a certain immaturity of some of the members on important questions. ("Ask Christoph, he will be able to explain. . . .") However, can it be any different in a community? Can everything really be gone into so minutely? Should not one rather give way in small things for the sake of progression and the higher goal?

Criticism and praise—my inner balance sheet is filled out with long columns—advantages weighed against disadvantages, pros and cons made clear. Which way do the scales incline?

But can we really do this? Can we just draw a line, add up the pros and cons, and then decide for one or the other? Do advantages and disadvantages really determine the decision for a way of life? No, if I simply set one point against another, I have not at all understood the life of these people. And I have not understood the Bible. A life of early Christian community, a life of complete dependence on God, is not a matter of the better of two possibilities. Whoever decides for it does not ask what advantages and disadvantages the life will bring. Whoever lives this life can do no other. They are gripped by God, called by him. They have to live this way, and they want to do so whatever the cost. The gain or the loss is not important to them. The quantity of pros and cons is not crucial; it is a matter of a quite different quality.

Mistakes and weaknesses, advantages and strong points of the bruderhof have nothing to say about the rightness of their life. I can decide only within myself whether I should live this way. This is a spiritual decision. Whoever tries to live this life in their own strength will soon lose strength. It is not a matter of finding a satisfying, alternate lifestyle, with community, early Christianity, and pacifism promoting a successful method. A little peace movement, a trip into ecumenism with mushy sympathies, love between people, garlands in the hair, and withdrawal into inwardness—all these do not make one into a Hutterite. Only those who have been gripped can live this way—those whom Christ has gripped—those who feel called and want to be obedient to this call. To come in this way to the bruderhof always also means to come to God.

To live this life means to be ready to suffer. It means surrendering oneself completely, abandoning one's plans, letting God alone decide everything, and trusting him. And I? Didn't I know this before living for two months on the bruderhof? Indeed I did. But these people *live* this life and take seriously all that which, until now, I have *said* that I believe. To do what one believes, to follow that which one has actually known for a long time to be right—that is what I lack again and again. I need this city on the hill, this bruderhof behind the seven mountains, this life that makes me homesick—for a different reality. Their witness gives me courage to dare and risk more, to serve more, to surrender myself.

We each need one another. The bruderhofs also need the experience of my churches back home. They need the courage of other Christians to avoid remaining in their own rut. They need the example of Christians who rely completely on Christ and daily ask God to speak anew to them from his living Word. We need the challenge that each one is to the other.

The most important experience of the bruderhof is something I already knew well long ago. But it became clearer here than in the normal everyday life of a parish. Forms—be they ever so radical—can never replace life. Even the most radical structures, early Christian lifestyles and the best community organizations, do not guarantee life. Community and pacifism, bruderhof or institutional church, of themselves do not bring me the least bit nearer to God. Community of goods does not liberate me from the urge for "me" and "mine." Only the Holy Spirit can do this. And he "blows where he wills" and is not bound by radical structures. Life does not exist in forms; life comes only from God.

Could I live like the members of the bruderhof? Everybody can. But no one can, without an active living relationship with the source of this life. No one can do it without daily surrender to the love of God. Only God is able to do away with all barriers and limitations. The revolutionary act that takes place in the heart is an inner experience. Community for life requires God's revolution within us every day.

Afterword

I do not like Forewords. Somehow, they get in my way when reading a book. Sometimes I get stuck at the Foreword, and then have no inclination to read the book itself. Oftentimes I heroically decide on the risky course of skipping the Foreword, in which case I ask myself three times in every chapter whether I have perhaps ignored the key to the book. So I have chosen to write an "Afterword." If you have come this far with me, you will manage a few more pages. I just want to tell you the circumstances under which this book was written.

My wife, Christel, and I were guests at Woodcrest bruderhof for about four weeks in the summer of 1983. During this time we spent a couple days at each of the other American bruderhofs. In the fall of 1984 we returned to Woodcrest for about three weeks. We also did some research in the community archives. All of the experiences described in this book are true. In writing about them I have changed only the order of events and in some cases a name, when it was no longer possible to identify it.

Without generous help from the bruderhof, this book could not have come into being. Not only were we received with much love and openness. We were given generous advice for this book, without any strings attached concerning the contents. During its preparation, a heartfelt friendship and feeling of oneness between us and the bruderhof arose.

We express our thanks particularly to our "old forester," Hermann Arnold, who set the pendulum swinging for the book and who cared for us like a father during our visits. Thanks also to the archive crew in Woodcrest: Hela, Winifred, and Miriam, and to Arnold and Gladys Mason, who left their desk to make room for me. Many good talks and good snacks link us to one another. It is in the nature of things that it is not possible to mention each one in such a large community in the way one would like to do. So we offer a collective "thank you" to all for hospitality and support, including the other bruderhofs, which do not appear much in this book but who played a real part in my picture of the communities.

A very special "thank you" is due my wife, Christel, for her moral support and partnership with me in writing this book. Her constructive criticism both annoyed and encouraged me. Her large share in writing, reading, remembering, and putting together was an enormous help. She could have participated more in the life of the community, but relinquished that option for long evenings of writing and brooding.

Many readers might ask what can still be seen today of the former community buildings in Germany. More than just a little. The first place at Sannerz is today a simple apartmenthouse in the village of Sannerz, near Schlüchtern. The inn owned by Lotzenius is still there on the opposite side of the road. The seven individual farms at the Sparhof that formed the Rhön bruderhof near Schlüchtern are often visited by young people from the current bruderhofs who go in quest of their roots in

Germany. The main house was severely damaged by artillery during World War II, and later was pulled down. The small burial ground which still belongs to the bruderhof lies on a small ridge a few hundred meters behind the Sparhof. The Alm bruderhof, Silum, has been returned to its former state as a mountain resort hotel a mile or so up in the Alps and is accessible to all.

A book of this kind can never tell all there is to say about a community. There is too much to write, much that I have forgotten or just not mentioned. A history of more than sixty years and the life of more than a thousand community members cannot be compressed into a small paperback. Much of what I have written can be understood only by trying to see it in the same spirit of love, humility, and submission to the Lord in whose footsteps the bruderhof people follow. Much will be better understood through a personal visit to the community. To serious questioners the doors of the bruderhof will gladly be opened. Addresses are found at the end of the book.

Anyone who would like to know more about the bruderhof is encouraged to read in the writings of Eberhard Arnold. It is worthwhile to explore further.

Finally, I'd like to express the hope that this book not be seen as merely the result of journalistic curiosity about a group of exotic dissenters. Rather, it is a book by one who feels spoken to and who, like many others, has a longing for a more convincing and fulfilled life.

The ultimate consideration, of course, is not a matter of Hutterianism, pacifism, or community of goods. All of us yearn for genuine fellowship and love. We are not able to achieve our ideals in our own strength. We must return to him through whom alone real life may be found.

Questions Asked of Prospective Novices

1. Are you certain that this way of brotherly community, based on a firm faith in God and Christ, is the way to which God has called you?

2. Are you ready to put yourself completely at the disposal of the church community of Christ to the end of your life—all your faculties, the whole strength of your body and soul, and your entire property, both that which you now possess and that which you may later inherit or earn?

3. Are you ready to accept every admonition (where this is justified) and, the other way around, to admonish others if you should sense within our community life something that should be clearer or would more fittingly bespeak the will of God, or if you should feel that something ought to be corrected or abolished?

4. Are you firmly determined to remain loyal and true, bound with us in mutual service as brothers and sisters, so that our love may be more burning and complete in the building of the church community, in the outreach to others, and in the proclamation of the gospel?

5. Are you ready then to surrender yourself completely and to bind yourself unreservedly to God, to Jesus Christ, and to the community?—Used in this form for the first time by Heini Arnold on December 2, 1953

Woodcrest

Hutterian Brethren
Rifton, New York

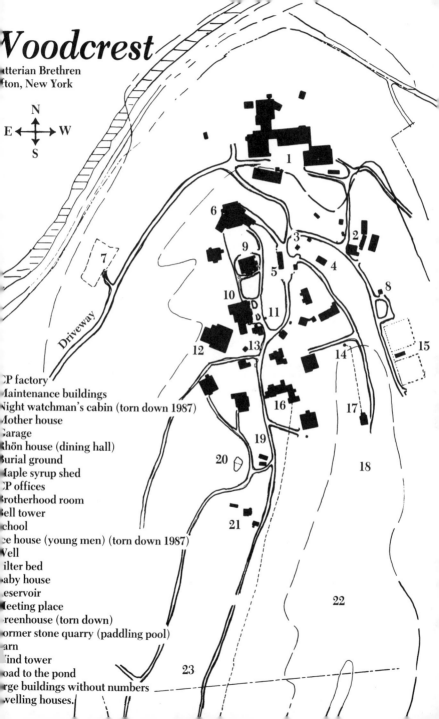

N
E ← → W
S

1. CP factory
2. Maintenance buildings
3. Night watchman's cabin (torn down 1987)
4. Mother house
5. Garage
6. Rhön house (dining hall)
7. Burial ground
8. Maple syrup shed
9. CP offices
10. Brotherhood room
11. Bell tower
12. School
13. Ice house (young men) (torn down 1987)
14. Well
15. Filter bed
16. Baby house
17. Reservoir
18. Meeting place
19. Greenhouse (torn down)
20. Former stone quarry (paddling pool)
21. Barn
22. Wind tower
23. Road to the pond

Large buildings without numbers
Dwelling houses.

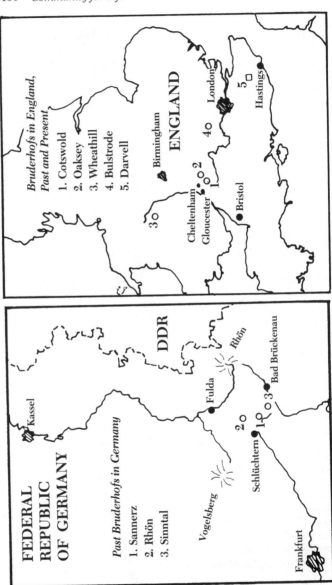

*Bruderhofs in England,
Past and Present*

1. Cotswold
2. Oaksey
3. Wheathill
4. Bulstrode
5. Darvell

ENGLAND

London
Birmingham
Cheltenham
Gloucester
Bristol
Hastings

FEDERAL
REPUBLIC
OF GERMANY

Past Bruderhofs in Germany

1. Sannerz
2. Rhön
3. Sinntal

DDR

Kassel
Rhön
Fulda
Bad Brückenau
Schlüchtern
Vogelsberg
Frankfurt

○ = Past   □ = Present day

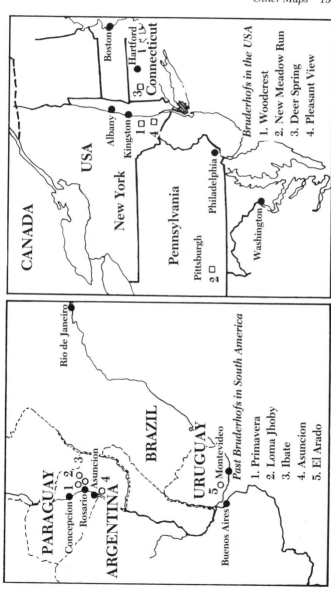

Bruderhofs in the USA

1. Woodcrest
2. New Meadow Run
3. Deer Spring
4. Pleasant View

CANADA

USA

New York

Pennsylvania

Boston
Hartford
Connecticut
Albany
Kingston
Philadelphia
Pittsburgh
Washington

Past Bruderhofs in South America

1. Primavera
2. Loma Jhoby
3. Ibate
4. Asuncion
5. El Arado

Rio de Janeiro

BRAZIL

PARAGUAY
ARGENTINA
URUGUAY

Concepcion
Rosario
Asuncion
Montevideo
Buenos Aires

○ = Past   □ = Present day

Time Line of the Bruderhofs

Sannerz (G)	1920——1927	
Rhön (G)	1926——1937	
Alm (Li)	1934——1938	
Cotswold (E)	1936——1941	
Oaksey (E)	1939-1941	
Primavera (P)	1941——1961	
Wheathill (E)	1942——1961	
Loma Jhoby (P)	1942——1961	
Asuncion (P)	1942——1961	
Ibate (P)	1947——1961	
El Arado (Ur)	1953——1960	
Woodcrest (USA)	1954——today	
Forest River (USA)	1955-1957	
Sinntal (G)	1955——1961	
(Oak Lake) New Meadow Run (USA)	1957——today	
Bulstrode (E)	1958——1966	
(Evergreen) Deer Spring (USA)	1958——today	
Darvell (E)	1971——today	
Pleasant View (USA)	1985——today	

For Further Reading

The Bruderhof: A Christian Community (Plough Publishing House)

16-page illustrated booklet in full color, telling briefly the history and aims of the bruderhof communities. (Also available in German, Spanish, Swedish, and French.)

Eberhard Arnold: A Testimony of Church Community from His Life and Writings (Plough Publishing House), 120 pages, cloth.

God's Revolution: The Witness of Eberhard Arnold edited by the Hutterian Brethren and John Howard Yoder (Paulist Press, 1984), 232 pages, paper.

Preface by Malcolm Muggeridge. Extracts on responding to the gospel as individuals, families, communal churches, and world citizens.

Hutterite Life by John A. Hostetler (Herald Press, 1983), 48 pages, paper.

An overview of the 300 colonies (with 30,000 people) in the United States and Canada, with full-color photographs.

Seeking for the Kingdom of God: Origins of the Bruderhof Communities by Eberhard and Emmy Arnold (Plough Publishing House), 240 pages, paper.

An account of the beginning, growth, and struggles of the bruderhof communities until 1937, when the Gestapo dissolved the Rhön bruderhof.

Youth Movement to Bruderhof: Letters and Diaries of Annemarie Arnold (nee Wärhter), 1926-1932 (Plough Publishing House), 256 pages, paper.

The housemother of four bruderhofs (1960-1980) tells of her search for meaning in life as a young person.

Plough Publishing House of the Hutterian Society of Brothers is located at Rifton, New York 12471; phone (914) 658-3141.

Hutterian Society of Brothers Addresses

Woodcrest Bruderhof, Rifton, New York 12471, USA

New Meadow Run Bruderhof, Farmington, Pennsylvania 15437, USA

Deer Spring Bruderhof, Norfolk, Connecticut 06058, USA

Darvell Bruderhof, Robertsbridge, East Sussex TN32 5 DR, England

Pleasant View Bruderhof, 300 Rosenthal Lane, Ulster Park, New York 12487, USA

Since 1979, Ulrich Eggers has been editor of *Punkt*, West Germany's leading monthly magazine for Christians between the ages of 18 and 40.

Born near Hamburg, he studied theology and geography at Hamburg University and completed a term of civil service.

Eggers was co-organizer of two large youth festivals in the Hamburg Congress Center featuring Christian music and arts, and speakers such as Ronald J. Sider.

Following two visits to the Woodcrest Bruderhof at Rifton, New York, he helped found *Weggemeinschaft* (Community of the Way) at Cuxhaven, where he serves as an elder of the group of 13 adults and 13 children.

The community operates a big youth holiday center on the coast as part of their social and missionary service. They remain active in the local congregation of the Free Evangelical Covenant Church.

Ulrich and Christel are the parents of Sonia and Laura.